Zen Guitar

philip toshio sudo

simon & schuster

Simon & Schuster
Rockefeller Center
1230 Avenue of the Americas
New York, NY 10020

Simon & Schuster and colophon are registered trademarks
of Simon & Schuster Inc.

Designed by Philip Toshio Sudo

Manufactured in the United States of America

10   9   8   7   6   5   4   3   2   1

Library of Congress Cataloging-in-Publication Data
Sudo, Philip Toshio.
Zen guitar / Philip Toshio Sudo.
p.   cm.
Includes bibliographical references.
1. Music—Philosophy and aesthetics.   2. Zen Buddhism.
3. Guitar.   I. Title.
ML3877.S8   1997
781'.1—dc20   96-42094
                                                    CIP
                                                    MN

ISBN 0-684-83090-6

Contents

PRACTICE
white belt to black belt 39

to

tracy, naomi,

and those yet unborn

道場

Dojo:
Place of the Way

the dojo

Welcome to the Zen Guitar Dojo. Please leave the door open.

My name is Philip Toshio Sudo, and I have established this dojo for anyone who wants to make music. It makes no difference to me whether you're a musician. You're welcome here if you're of the spirit to make a sound.

I began playing the guitar as a child in Japan, the land of my ancestors, and have continued playing in the United States, the land of my birth. Over the years I've learned from many different teachers, both Japanese and American. As the product of these two cultures, I've sought a way to blend the wisdom of East and West into a universal philosophy of life.

The way I've found is Zen Guitar.

Zen Guitar is nothing more than playing the song we're all

born with inside—the song that makes us human. Any one of us can do it. The music is waiting there to be unlocked.

This dojo will give you the key.

My intention here is to share what I've learned in the hope it might encourage you to strum a new song in the world.

As the name implies, *Zen Guitar* is based largely on the principles of zen philosophy. Zen is most easily understood as a commonsense approach to all things. Some people come to know zen through meditation, others through the martial arts, or archery, or flower arranging. All these are paths to the same wisdom.

Zen

Here we seek to know zen through music.

I named this the *Zen Guitar Dojo* because it is a place of work

Dojo

and contemplation. *Dojo* is a Japanese word meaning, literally, "Place of the Way"—the ultimate Way of life and death that governs nature and the universe. It is through our endeavors in the dojo that we discover the Way.

A good dojo is like a school, practice hall, and temple rolled into one. The aim is to train body, mind, and spirit together, at the same time.

You can make a dojo anywhere. Just as a believer does not need a house of worship to pray, a student of music needs no special place to play Zen Guitar. A bedroom, basement, garage, porch, or street corner will serve just fine. All that's required to make a dojo is the proper frame of mind.

My approach to the guitar brings in various teachings from the zen arts of Asia: martial arts such as karate and aikido, brush-style calligraphy, samurai swordsmanship, and the Japanese tea ceremony. As in the tradition of these great arts, I believe that learning to play the guitar is inseparable from learning to harmonize body, mind, and spirit. To truly play from your soul, you must have all aspects of yourself working together as one.

As you develop this harmony, it will carry through to everything you do. In other words, what you learn in this dojo will apply to your work, school, athletics, relationships, home life—how you think, see, feel, and hear all day long. Because ultimately, the path of Zen Guitar is the path of life itself.

This dojo is for beginners and advanced students alike, with no distinction made for age or past experience. Anyone who wants to train here, regardless of ability, starts at the same point: wearing the white belt, just as one would in studying a martial art. Even a black belt in karate, for example, must put on a white belt when beginning the study of another martial art like judo. It is no different here, no matter how long you've been playing or who your other teachers have been.

Donning the white belt does not mean you are a novice,

though there is no shame in being one. In fact, in many ways, novices have an advantage over those who come from other schools and may have to unlearn certain ways of thinking. Wearing the white belt merely signifies that you are willing to learn the Way of Zen Guitar.

You should know from the beginning that Zen Guitar is not a conventional how-to program of instruction. It is *alternative,* meaning it requires a do-it-yourself spirit. There are no chords or tunings or music theory in this dojo; you won't find lessons on how to read music, play the blues, fingerpick, or copy "Stairway to Heaven." All of that is *information.* Information is something you can get from a gamut of sources—magazines, books, classes, friends, videos, computer networks. The world is swimming in information. Any student with enough dedication knows how to acquire information.

But information alone cannot teach you what you need to know to play your song. At the Zen Guitar Dojo, our aim is not to acquire information but wisdom. The idea here is to train and to experience; it is only through the experience of our senses that we truly gain wisdom. One cannot learn Zen Guitar simply by reading. Just as no words can teach us how to ride a bicycle, the only way we can learn to play our song is through the direct experience of our bodies. To learn through experience—that is the path of Zen Guitar. There is a zen saying, "Paths cannot be taught, they can only be taken." So it is with Zen Guitar.

My function here will be to act as your guide. I do so in the spirit of the Japanese *sensei*—not "teacher," as the word is commonly translated but, literally, "one who has gone before." I do not claim to know all the answers. But what I have learned, I'll gladly share with those who wish to make a

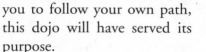

Sensei

similar journey. If I can inspire you to follow your own path, this dojo will have served its purpose.

Unsui

Those who train here I regard not as students, but *unsui*. In Japanese, unsui means traveling monk or truth-seeker. Literally, it translates as "cloud and water." To be an unsui is to embody the spirit of Zen Guitar—floating, flowing, at once with and without form. If you learn to view yourself in this way, your journey on the path of Zen Guitar will have no end.

Beginning students often ask, "How long will it take me to learn the Way of Zen Guitar?" My answer is, as long as you live—that short. Your playing may progress enough to impress your friends in a year's time, perform onstage in two years, or turn professional in three. But if those are the ends you seek, your concern is not Zen Guitar. The Way of Zen Guitar is learned day by day, minute by minute, second by second, now to eternity. There is no faster way.

Beginning students also commonly ask, "How long until I get my black belt?" To them I say, you'll never earn a black belt so long as you ask that question. To be obsessed with the destination is to remove the focus from where you are. The only way to progress in Zen Guitar is to put everything into this step, right now.

While it's true that in some schools a student formally graduates from one belt level to the next, in the Zen Guitar Dojo there is no such graduation. Students here receive one belt and one belt only: the white belt. Those who put in the time, training, and effort will find their belt getting so soiled that eventually it turns black of its own accord. Only then will they have achieved black-belt status.

In Zen Guitar, the black belt is not a goal or an end anyway. At other schools, the black belt may signify ultimate achievement, but in Zen Guitar it is only a point along the path. I have great respect for those who reach the black-belt level; it takes sincere commitment. But the true Way of Zen Guitar asks black-belt players to redouble their training until their belt becomes so worn and frayed it begins to lose color and returns to white. Only through completion of that circle—white to black, black to white—can one know the depth of the Way.

Thus, I have divided my teaching into five stages, each signifying progression along the path of Zen Guitar.

The first stage, *White Belt,* establishes the proper mindset for starting out on the path—a mindset the student must maintain every step thereafter. This is what's called the *beginner's mind.*

The second stage, *White Belt to Black Belt,* describes the kind of training and discipline needed to progress along the path. This is the work ethic one must maintain through all stages of growth. In this section I also warn of some common missteps that can lead one astray no matter how hard the training.

The third stage, *Black Belt,* explains the standard required for excellence, as well as the responsibilities. It describes the kind of thinking, feeling, and attitude required of a black belt. This is the level where body, mind, and spirit begin to fuse.

The fourth stage, *Black Belt to White Belt,* explores the barrier that lies beyond technical excellence and leads to a deeper understanding of the Way.

The last stage, *White Belt,* reveals the true Way of Zen Guitar.

I encourage students to think of these stages as broadly as possible. You may be a novice in the world of sound, but you're not a novice in life. Most likely, you're a black belt in some other area—carpentry, law, cooking, computer programming, skiing, whatever. Use that knowledge to understand the Way of Zen Guitar, and your training in Zen Guitar will take your existing skills to an even higher level.

Those of you already skilled in music can benefit from training here as well. I hear many guitarists with talent who seem to lack direction, who can't articulate a reason for doing what they do. The Way of Zen Guitar gives those players a sense of purpose. Not only that, it provides a framework from which to tackle any new task. Once you learn the principles of Zen Guitar, you can apply them to any endeavor outside music. Follow the samurai maxim that says, "From one thing, know ten thousand things." Music can teach you everything you need to know.

If you're wondering when the discussion will turn to zen philosophy, don't concern yourself. Put your entire focus into playing the guitar. If you do that, in time your questions will answer themselves.

For anyone who wants to leave now, thank you for your interest. You are always welcome to return—there is never a time when you cannot begin. The door to this dojo is always open.

For those of you who choose to stay, please put on the white belt. You have taken the first step on the path. ○

Shiro: White

beginner's mind

My own thing is in my head. I hear sounds and if I don't get them together nobody else will.

——Jimi Hendrix

"Why have you come to this place at this time?" When I ask this question, students often say they don't know; they just want to play guitar. There are those who see the guitar as a means to build their self-esteem—to attract the girls or, as the case may be, the boys. Others say they already know their way around the guitar and are just curious to see what goes on here.

Whatever your personal reason for coming, I believe there's an ultimate reason we're in this dojo, one that applies to all who set foot through these doors:

We are here to make a sound.

Maybe this sound is one we first heard someone else make, a sound that spoke to us or moved us in some profound way. Every guitar player has a story like this to tell. Maybe the sound is so big it swells up inside naturally and comes bursting forth like springwater. Inside your head, the sound is so good, you've got to play it out loud just to hear it. Maybe you're searching and don't even know what the sound *is*, you just know what it is not. Some of us feel so strongly about the sound that we've got to play it for others, sharing it as though passing a flame from candle to candle.

This dojo exists for that sound—to discover it, celebrate it and, most of all, to make it.

Sekishu no onjo

I hear many students ask, "What exactly is this sound? A Gibson Les Paul through a stack of Marshall amps? A hand-crafted classical played center stage at Carnegie Hall?"

It is all of that and none of that. At bottom, it is the sound of the divine spark within us all. Like the cry of a child or the howl of a wolf, it transcends language and culture. It is the sound that drives the dance of life. Zen masters call it *sekishu no onjo*—"the sound of one hand clapping."

Each of us has the potential to know this sound in our own way. Some people are driven to find it through bongos or bagpipes, others use kalimbas or keyboards. Some just open their throats and sing. Some hear the sound through dance or diving or acting or architecture—or just sitting in complete silence.

It's not enough to simply find your means to express this sound, though sadly, some people never do. You must find your sound, then dig into it until you reach its very source. This is the challenge of Zen Guitar. For at the source of your sound is the source of all sound. Digging to that source means learning to hear every sound—yours and all those around you—as both distinct and One Great Sound. Call it the sound of one hand clapping, call it the voice of God. If you get to that source you will know the answer to every question because you will have heard it all.

Whatever obstacles you face, never stop listening to the sound inside you. Do so and you are sure to lose the Way.

Now, if you are ready to proceed, all you ever need do on the path of Zen Guitar is this:

1. Wear the white belt.
2. Pick up your guitar.
3. Tune.
4. Play.

Dedicate yourself to understanding the true meaning of these four steps and you are sure to find the Way of Zen Guitar. Go down the path as far as you can, but never lose sight of the beginning. In the end, the purity and openness of the white belt is where you want to return.

Wear the White Belt

Whenever I start working on a song, I immediately try to forget everything, to empty my hands and head of anything that may be hanging over from another song or album. I try to approach it like, "This is the first time I've ever played a guitar. What am I going to do?"

—The Edge, U2

White belt in this dojo signifies the spirit of beginning. No matter how adept you are with the guitar already, wearing the white belt here means you have agreed to set aside all knowledge and preconceptions and open your mind to learning as though for the first time.

In zen circles, this attitude is called *carrying an empty cup*. It stems from an oft-repeated parable about the visit of a university professor to the home of a nineteenth-century zen master named Nan-in. The professor had come to inquire about zen but in conversation, he spent more time talking than listening. In response, Nan-in began pouring the professor's tea until it flowed out of the cup and onto the table.

"What are you doing!" the professor exclaimed.

"Like this cup, you are full of your own ideas," replied the master. "How can I teach unless you first empty your cup?"

When we empty our cup, we agree to rid ourselves of the preconceptions that block new learning. This is the attitude of the true beginner, the mind required to know Zen Guitar.

In this dojo, I've tried to distill each lesson down to its essence. Look upon each lesson as a small bag of tea. To consume the teaching, pour in your own hot water. That is, seek to relate what I say to your own experience and provide examples from your own life. That way, the teaching will have more resonance for you. Words can only guide you. Your bones have to understand.

From here on out, drink and keep an empty cup. The moment you think you know everything there is to know, you will have lost the way. The beginner's mind is the mind of wisdom.

Pick Up Your Guitar

If you pick up a guitar and it says, "Take me, I'm yours," then that's the one for you.

———Frank Zappa

"Pick up your guitar" means two things in this dojo. First, for those of you who do not yet have a guitar, it means to go into the world and find the instrument that's waiting for you, the one you are meant to play. Electric with effects, acoustic with gut strings—it doesn't matter. There's an instrument for everyone. What's important is that when you pick it up, it makes a sound that's beautiful to you.

When conducting your search, make sure you look for an instrument of suitable quality. This goes for any additional equipment required to make your sound: amplifier, pickups, pedals, and so on. Avoid poor craftsmanship; it's the sign of a poor spirit. That doesn't mean you have to buy the most expensive equipment. It just means you want something suitable for your designs.

Learn to identify quality and appreciate anything that's well made, wherever you find it. Look deeply into the spirit that goes into making an item of quality—the care, the precision, the attention to detail. Incorporate that spirit into your work in this dojo. Anything you set out to make—music, love, a bookshelf, a meal—make as well as you can. To do otherwise is spiritless.

If you can't yet afford the quality you want, make do until you can. Your main concern is learning to make sound. The first-time driver does not need a Ferrari to learn how to drive; any car that moves will do. I have seen one-string guitars constructed out of broom handles and wire, and drum kits assembled from paint buckets and trash-can lids. If the sound within you is strong, it will find a way to come out.

The second thing I mean by "pick up your guitar" concerns the way you physically take it in your hands. Don't pick up your guitar aimlessly. Act with a sense of purpose. Be of the mind that you're going to *do* something—even if you don't know what that is yet. Prepare yourself to play.

Maybe you just want to noodle on it while watching TV. Then pick up your guitar *with the mind of* noodling while watching TV. Remember, the guitar is an instrument—a thing by means of which something is done. Keep this in mind every time you reach for it.

When you pick it up, *pick it up*.

Tune

I [write] by twiddling the strings into a different tuning—I throw it open to the cosmos. Then when you discover something that has an element of divine intervention, it's like a blessing.
——Joni Mitchell

Before playing a note, we all need to learn how to get in tune and to stay in tune. It's good to think broadly about this as it relates to all aspects of playing.

To tune means to bring into harmony. On the most basic level, we have to bring our instrument into harmony with itself. The majority of players use a standard tuning that offers the widest range of expressive possibilities. But any tuning can work for Zen Guitar, however unconventional. If a tuning feels right for just one person or one song, all the rules of music don't matter. Zen Guitar can manifest itself through any sound if the player has the correct spirit.

Some beginners find it easy to tune their instrument; others struggle with tuning for months. There is no trick or technique involved in tuning. If you find it difficult to tune, stick with it. Patience and concentration will be vital attributes as you move along the path. Combat discouragement with your desire to learn. You cannot know Zen Guitar if you insist on instant gratification.

Tuning means learning to *hear*. Too many of us allow our eyes to dominate our ears. Try closing your eyes and listening with the ears of a blind person. Lessen your reliance on one sense and the other senses will grow stronger.

Anyone who can tell the chirp of a bird from the bark of a dog can distinguish a higher pitch from a lower pitch and, thus, learn to tune. In time, with proper listening and experience, the ear becomes sensitive enough to distinguish even between sounds that are very similar, just as the eyes can distinguish between similar shades of blue. Notice how a mother can distinguish the cry of her baby from that of another. Learn to hear in the same way and you will have no problems tuning.

Beyond tuning the instrument itself, it's also important for you to be in tune *with* the instrument. In the same way that singers understand their own voices, learn to understand your guitar. Every guitar has its own feel and idiosyncrasies, the same way a car does. Different guitars will lead you to different songs. Pick up a Rickenbacker twelve-string and one kind of song comes out; pick up a Fender Telecaster and another kind comes out. When you're in tune with your instrument, you're open to receiving these songs.

Much more difficult on the path of Zen Guitar is finding an internal tuning—one that brings body, mind, and spirit into harmony. A player must be clear of internal static such as impatience and frustration; otherwise, the spirit frizzles like a radio slightly off dial. Your sound must have what the Chinese call *ch'iyun*: a sympa-

气
原

Ch'iyun

thetic vibration of the vital spirit. It is a harmony that speaks from your heart directly to the heart of the listener—an intangible element that enables us to transcend our separateness and feel the greater oneness. Learn to recognize ch'iyun in the music that inspires you, in your favorite paintings, when watching a great dancer or athlete. When you feel that moment of transcendence, where your spirit is uplifted—that's what we're going for.

One more note about tuning as it relates to playing with other people: Tuning is an absolute requirement for functioning as a collective. It is the common ground where players of any culture can meet. Think of tuning as it relates to all human interaction, on both an individual and societal level. How many bands have broken up for reasons that have nothing to do with music, because they cannot get along together? How many marriages, teams, legislatures, boards, and committees fail to function because the participants can't find a working harmony? When people are not in tune with each other, they add to the disharmony of the world.

Sometimes, the only way to attune to others is through compassion, courage, and selflessness. Such is the difficult path of Zen Guitar.

A famous zen story describes the depth of what it means to be so in tune. It relates the experience of a monk named Ryokan, who returned home one night to find a thief.

Living an ascetic life, Ryokan had nothing in his home worth stealing. But he surprised the intruder, saying, "You may have come a long way to visit me and you should not return empty-handed. Please take my robe as a gift."

He offered forth the robe from his back, and the thief slunk away.

"Poor fellow," the master said, gazing at the night sky. "I wish I could give him this beautiful moon."

To find such harmony within ourselves, with others, with all of nature—this is what it means to think broadly about tuning.

Play

*A nonmusician is thrilled to be doing music and is quite happy to
sit there and plunk one note all day. And is very alert to the effect
of that. Nonmusicians really* listen *sometimes, because that's the
only thing they have available to them.*

——Brian Eno

O nce you have tied on the white belt, picked up your guitar, and tuned, you need only to play.

"What?" you say. "I'm just a beginner, I don't know any
songs or even how to play at all!" Here is where you start: Play
one note on one string and *pour in every ounce of your heart and
soul.* Then repeat.

On a technical level, any beginner can do this. The challenge
is one of spirit. The idea is the same as the tennis coach who instructs beginners to hit the ball as hard as they can with no concern for whether the ball lands in court or not. First learn the
feeling of hitting the ball hard; worry about accuracy later. Zen
Guitar is like this.

If you can't play what you hear, then *hear what you play.* The
intensity of your effort should be the same as if
you were shouting from your gut at the waves
crashing ashore. Martial arts call this kind of
shout *katsu.* Katsu is the roar of a person who
knows what it means to be alive.

Take note of how martial artists shout when they

喝

Katsu

34 beginner's mind

kick or throw a punch in training. This kind of shouting builds spirit. Note, too, that the shout and the strike are not two separate things; they are one thing. Try bringing the same spirit to guitar playing.

If you sweat hard and build your strength from one note up, you'll begin to see progress. After one note, play two notes together; then three. Learn a chord, then a second and a third. If you can play three chords with maximum spirit, you have all the elements you need to make real music. The guitar has shown us again and again: Three chords can rock the world.

Most of all, play with joy. Therein you'll find the Way.

As I said before, Zen Guitar is not a conventional method. My concern is not so much the "how" of guitar playing as the "why." The Way of Zen Guitar is to express the spirit through music, regardless of experience, equipment, or even technique. That's not to downplay the need for good technique. But in this school, one acquires technique solely for the purpose of freeing the spirit. Technique is not an end in itself. Your spiritual approach to playing is more important in this dojo than what you actually play or the technique with which you play it.

After all, Zen Guitar is not a style of playing. Rock, jazz, blues, country, classical, avant garde—it doesn't matter. They're all rivers that lead to the same ocean. What's important is to play from the heart and soul. If you do that, you'll have no need to search for a personal style or signature sound; it will develop naturally. Uniqueness is something inborn, like a fingerprint. Your playing style in Zen Guitar should come from the inside out, not the outside in.

If you really want to learn Zen Guitar, you can. It is not the same as, say, wanting to play professional basketball, where one can fail to make the team for lack of natural talent. Zen Guitar is more like running a marathon. Those who want to run, run. Those determined to finish, finish. As the samurai say, "The only opponent is within." There are no tricks or secrets. It is a matter of will—putting one foot in front of the other every step of the path. In Zen Guitar, honesty, integrity, spiritual strength, and depth of conviction are more important than skill. These are the elements that make vital music, and they have nothing to do with natural talent. Where there's a will, there's the Way.

Play on. Your belt is getting soiled. ○

Shiro-Kuro: White-Black

practice

It takes a lot of devotion and work, or maybe I should say play, because if you love it, that's what it amounts to. I haven't found any shortcuts, and I've been looking for a long time.

——Chet Atkins

Most of us are lucky if we qualify as experts at one thing in our lives. Expertise does not come easily; often, it does not come at all. Many people lack the will and discipline required to get good at something.

The purpose of this dojo is to provide a training ground for those people who have the will and discipline to know the Way of Zen Guitar. The Japanese call this kind of practice *shugyo*—literally, mastering one's deeds. Understand that for as long as you follow the path of Zen Guitar, you will be in shugyo. There will never come a point where practicing ends, even should you reach the black-belt level or beyond. The path of Zen Guitar goes on forever.

But do not feel overwhelmed by the length of

Shugyo

this journey. All you ever need do is focus on one thing: what you are doing. Stay on the path and put one foot in front of the other—that is all. There is joy in the struggle.

Once you have picked up the guitar, tuned it, and started playing, you need to establish a pattern for training. How you do this is up to you. You may develop your own training regimen or follow one of the many structured programs developed by other teachers. If there is a particular style you want to play, find a teacher or a book to show it to you. If your hearing is good, listen and learn it yourself. Work from models. Copy the licks on your favorite records. These songs have already given you the feeling you want to convey. Use them as roadmaps to finding your own sound. So many different formulas can work that there's no real formula. What's important is to learn from whomever or whatever you can, at your own rate, in your own way. How or when you learn doesn't matter, so long as the learning occurs.

To guide your training during this intermediate stage between white belt and black belt, I have divided the teaching into two sections:

1. The Twelve Points of Focus.
2. The Twelve Common Missteps.

The Twelve Points of Focus are those areas where you should concentrate your early training. Human beings being creatures of habit, it is best to establish the proper approach to shugyo right away. Habit gives us comfort; it is familiar. In this dojo, you must develop comfort in good habits. You need not try to change everything you find wrong with yourself. Start with one new habit: *Do one thing the right way one time.* When the next moment comes, make the same commitment. If you do this, the bad habits will take care of themselves.

Think about each point as it relates to the way you practice and the way you live. Let these points guide your playing and progress, and they will help you stay on the path of Zen Guitar.

The Twelve Common Missteps are potholes along the path that every player must work to avoid at every point. Endeavoring to know the Way demands moment-to-moment vigilance. In one small detail, we can deviate from the path. If left unchecked, these deviations can, over time, lead to a wide divergence from the path. Like the alcoholic who says, "I'll only have this one drink this one time," many unsui think they are on the right track when they actually have fallen off it. For some people, that "one drink" may be an excuse to skip practice; a year later, the guitar is shrouded in dust and cobwebs. Selfishness, egotism, laziness—a single act can lead to a long detour. You must check your path constantly and make corrections as you go. Failure to acknowledge these missteps can lead one far astray.

If you maintain the Twelve Points of Focus and guard against the Twelve Common Missteps, you are doing all you can do. Carry them with you the whole of your life and you will flow in every endeavor.

The Twelve Points of Focus

Spirit
Rhythm
Technique
Feel
Perfection
Mistakes
Stages and Plateaus
Discipline
Limits
Follow-Through
Taste
Collaboration

Spirit

"Yeaaaah," he says, fingering the valves, "when she gets broken in, a few weeks down the road, this is going to be a nice horn."

"Sounds like she blows real easy, Diz."

He fixes me with a stagey stare. "Sheeeeeet. Ain't none of them blow easy."

——Chip Stern, relating a conversation with Dizzy Gillespie

Guitar playing is a physical activity that demands training. In that sense it is no different than learning to throw a discus, run the high hurdles, or swim the butterfly. The body must acquire an intelligence of its own. The muscles must learn to move in new and disciplined ways.

Physical challenges force the mind to confront obstacles: pain, fatigue, self-doubt. You cannot make progress on the path without developing some kind of mental strength. Use your training here to build a strong spirit.

When the body engages in something new, it forces the mind to pay attention—to acquire focus, direction, and resolve. Conversely, when the body tires of an activity, the mind must forge discipline and endurance in the muscles. Beginning guitar players, for example, often complain of painful fingertips from pressing down on the strings. Right away, the mind must teach the hands to fight through this discomfort until calluses build. As any jogger knows, when the body wants to quit, the mind has to step in and say no.

Frustration results when the body will not perform as the mind directs, or the mind becomes confused about what it wants the body to do. These confrontations between mind and body are an integral part of training. They bring us face to face with our motivations and limitations: Why are we putting in all these hours of practice? Why do we desire what we desire? Are we willing to make the sacrifice necessary to progress? Are we asking more of our body than it can do? How we answer these questions determines our progress along the path of Zen Guitar.

Your spirit here must be one of total resolution; as martial artists like to say, "Tighten your mind." You may arrive here like a wild colt, scattered and unfocused. Through training, learn to harness your raw energy and charge like a racehorse. Other beginners arrive with the spirit of a tired nag. Through training, they learn to build up their energy the way one strengthens a little-used muscle.

Here are three adages from the samurai on the spirit required to know the Way. Fix these in your heart as you train:

1. Don't ask, practice.

Some questions no one can answer but yourself. Practice properly and the answers will come to you in time. The only route to understanding the Way is through your own experience.

2. Seven times down, eight times up.

If you slip in your training, get up. Even should you think defeatist thoughts—"I can't learn this," "My hands aren't strong enough," "I'll never be any good"—never voice them aloud. Burn such thoughts from your mind before you make a single utterance.

The famed martial artist Bruce Lee was said to have done that exact thing: Whenever a negative thought came into his head, he would visualize writing the words down on a slip of paper and putting it to flames.

Apply this thinking to your own training.

3. The only opponent is within.

What matters on the path of Zen Guitar is not the obstacles we face but how we respond to them. Master your reaction to the unforeseen and unfortunate circumstance, and you will master the Way of Zen Guitar.

When you are focused on the Way, every physical task becomes the object of mental training, no matter how small. Washing the dishes, making the bed, mowing the lawn—at every opportunity, keep your mind from laziness and wandering. Pay attention to the task at hand and it will carry over into everything you do. This is the spirit required to know the Way of Zen Guitar.

Rhythm

The focus of my playing is the groove, and every time I find a new rhythm, I find I can write a bunch of new songs. Learning how to dance, or drum, or to swing my body in a new way is the fundamental way I find a new riff. Because when you learn to swing your body in a new way, you begin to swing with your instrument differently.

—Stone Gossard, Pearl Jam

I often hear people say they have no natural rhythm. This is false. Anyone with a heartbeat has rhythm. Anyone who breathes in and breathes out has rhythm. Anyone who walks has rhythm. The important thing is to feel it and put it in your music.

One of the Japanese words for rhythm, *hyoshi*, translates literally as "child's clap." This is the sense of rhythm you must feel—as natural as the handclap of a child.

拍子

Hyoshi

Zen Guitar does not require you to play to any rhythm but your own. But you should develop the ability to align your rhythm with other rhythms—to *feel the groove*. We all have this in-born ability. Notice at the end of a concert how the crowd cheers for an encore. Initially, each member of the audience claps in his or her own rhythm. But then the whole room locks into the same rhythm and claps in unison. This is hyoshi on a group level.

You can find hyoshi in everything—the change of the seasons, the cycle of the moon, the measure of night to day; the movement of the tides, high and low; within the tides, in the sets of waves; in each wave as it washes and recedes from shore. There is hyoshi outside of nature as well, in the man-made click-clack of a windshield wiper, ring of the telephone, or spin of the washing machine. There is hyoshi in the abstract, in notions such as beauty, space, and lifestyle. There is hyoshi in human relations, in the vibe we give to each other. There is hyoshi in the places we live, in the feel of streets and neighborhoods, towns and cities.

You must learn to feel hyoshi overlapping in every facet of your life and bring it to all that you play. Basketball players often speak of wanting to shoot the ball "in rhythm," meaning within the flow of the game. In other words, they want their actions to arise *naturally*. This is hyoshi.

Learn to feel the hyoshi of numbers, too. Those students inclined to mathematics should feel a close affinity to the order of music. Music is full of mathematics—scales, beats, time, and sonic frequencies all have a mathematical component. Know the subdivisions of numbers; know the rhythm between the numbers. Above all, always feel the one, whether it's at the top of the beat or the bottom of your soul.

Remember, you cannot feel rhythm with your mind; you must feel it in your body. When you physically repeat a pattern enough times—no matter how basic or complex—you will inhabit that pattern with your soul.

If your spirit is large enough, you can sense hyoshi even in things that are seemingly arrhythmic. All things have an underlying pulse, and their source is the same.

There is nothing deeper than this on the path of Zen Guitar.

Technique

The music has generated all the techniques I use. When I sit down to learn to play something . . . it is not because I want to master a technique. It is because I want to hear what an idea sounds like.

——Pat Martino

Some teachers build entire programs around the acquisition of technique. There are schools of fingerpicking, schools of slide guitar, and schools of two hands on the fretboard. Without question, technique is essential to know, especially if you desire to play a certain style. But you will not learn the Way of Zen Guitar solely through technique.

In Zen Guitar, the acquisition of technique for its own sake is not the path to musicianship. The expression is the thing, whatever the means. If you want to spend hours and hours practicing your technique, do so; by necessity, we all must spend time there. But the more complicated the technique, the more attention your mind must give to it. The aim here is to play without having to think about technique. One's main focus should be on playing with the proper spirit.

Technique is what enables us to articulate with efficiency and clarity. But first we must have something to say. Sometimes a player with crude technique has more to say than a player with impeccable technique. Whose song is more uplifting?

Acquire only the technique you need, and no more. That is the Way of Zen Guitar.

Feel

*You know, I've done a [drum] clinic in L.A. Nice kids, but they
all asked the same question, this, "How did you work out that
fill?" I told them, "I don't know." I don't know. I feel it, it's that
particular day, who knows? . . . Just play. Let your personality
come out.*

———Manu Katché, drummer, Peter Gabriel band

Many beginners think that in order to play music, they
must first learn how to read it. In this dojo, it's more
important to feel it.

Unquestionably, learning to read and write musical notation
deepens one's understanding of music the same way that, say,
learning Japanese deepens one's appreciation for Japan. By
knowing the written language of music, composers can communicate to players across the ages and record their music
without the need for sound.

Reading and writing does not, however, give a person any advantage on the path of Zen Guitar. To say someone can play a
score of Mozart's means no more than saying an actor can recite
the lines of Shakespeare. What's important is not the ability to
read, but the soul and emotion a player brings to the work. Two
actors can read the same lines of a play, but one may do a better
job of creating a living, breathing character. So it is with music.
More than knowing and playing the correct notes, the sound

must have a *feel*—a human pulse that resonates to all within earshot.

Having the right feel is not simply a matter of technique; as they say in the theater world, if you notice how good the acting is, it's not good acting. It is a matter of having ch'iyun, a sympathetic vibration of the vital spirit.

The Way of Zen Guitar is known through the ears and the heart, not the rational mind. A self-taught blues player from the Mississippi Delta can know the Way of Zen Guitar where a graduate of Julliard may be lost. The Way is found in the spirit of the expression and its depth, not its complexity. Do not allow knowledge to interfere with the naturalness that music demands. One can easily overthink a part. Just play. If it feels right, it *is* right.

Perfection

I don't think you can ever do your best. Doing your best is a process of trying to do your best.

—Townes Van Zandt

T he point of training is to strive for perfection. Just as the golfer seeks to strike the ball perfectly with each swing of the club, so should the guitar player intend to play each note perfectly.

The reason we value perfection is for its very difficulty to attain. Being human, mistakes are unavoidable. But that is no excuse to accept mistakes lightly. If each member of a quintet were to say, "Well, I made only one mistake on that take," the recording would have five mistakes and they'd all be back to the top. So be of the mind to play perfectly every time.

Many mistakes arise from self-consciousness—from too much focus on what the body is actually doing. When pitching a baseball, throwing a football, or shooting a basketball, problems always arise when the athlete tries to *aim* the ball. So it is with playing guitar. When the mind becomes preoccupied with what the hands are doing, it shuts out the music inside.

The only way to overcome self-consciousness is through practice. With practice our muscles develop their own intelligence, to the point where thought and action occur simultaneously. Our skill becomes natural—part of what zen masters call our *ordinary mind.*

The progression toward this naturalness is no different than when we first learn skills like driving or typing. As beginning drivers, we feel terribly self-conscious, awkwardly checking the mirrors, turning too wide, braking too suddenly. Similarly, when we first learn to type, our fingers move very deliberately on the keyboard, each move requiring careful thought.

With practice, though, our muscles no longer rely on the mind. Behind the wheel, the foot starts to move naturally between brake and gas. At the keyboard, fingers fly to the correct letters without conscious direction. In time, these actions become as ordinary as walking.

Practice alone does not make perfect, though. As a renowned baseball instructor once said, "*Perfect* practice makes perfect." This is the attitude required to know the Way of Zen Guitar.

Mistakes

If you hit a wrong note, then make [it] right by what you play afterwards.

——Joe Pass

In life, a single mistake can result in death. Running through a red light just once can do it. But in the realm of Zen Guitar, mistakes can lead to a kind of rebirth.

The spirit of Zen Guitar is to learn from mistakes as soon as they happen and salvage them by incorporating them into the artistic process. Try this in your playing: After hitting a wrong note accidentally, *play the same note again like you really mean it.* As a guitarist friend of mine put it, learn how to turn a wince into a smile.

You must take care not to make mistakes. But when they happen, learn from them. Use your mistakes as a springboard into new areas of discovery; accidents can hold the key to innovation.

When things fall apart, make art. Carry this spirit through to every area of your life.

Stages and Plateaus

I'm only 49 years old. I'm still in the middle of this whole thing.
I don't feel like it's finished at all. I'm still planning to write
better songs.

—Paul McCartney

The path of Zen Guitar is like scaling a wall with no visible top. To progress, think like a rock climber. At times it may become necessary to move laterally before moving upward. At other times it may be necessary to rest and regroup, or even move down a step, before continuing. Remember, a pattern of two steps up, one step back is still progress. Do not think of these moves as anything other than part of your overall path of advancement. Sometimes you attack, other times you tack. The spirit is always the same; only the strategy differs.

Over the long haul, the path of development consists of stages and plateaus. The dedicated beginner will see rapid improvement in the early going, but after a while the rate of improvement will taper off. We can work and work and work and not see any progress. Then suddenly, we move up to a new stage of ability, as though arriving in a meadow clearing out of a jungle.

Be aware that the farther on the path you go, the longer the plateaus get. During these times, you may feel like you're in a rut. The way out is to stay focused on your training—what you are doing *right now*. Don't look ahead to where you want to be, and don't look back thinking, "I've only come this far." If you put in an honest effort, you will break through to the next level. You can't make long-term progress conform to your timetable. It has to happen naturally. A flower blooms when it's ready to bloom. Let it be.

When arriving at a new stage, do not think your difficulties will vanish, either. Each level of achievement brings a new set of problems. This should be understood beforehand.

Whatever you do, move only at a pace that is natural. Do not concern yourself with those who seem to pass you by. On the path of Zen Guitar, there is no last train out of town—no destination, no deadlines. If some folks want to rush by you, let them go. Where they're heading is not the Way.

So long as your spirit keeps going forward, you're moving fast enough.

Discipline

It takes a lot of discipline to be very proficient on your instrument. . . . [Y]ou have to really exercise your willpower . . . reach down really deep within and pull out stuff you never knew you had, strength you never bothered to find before.

—Steve Vai

The key to self-mastery lies in discipline. Discipline governs how we train, when we train, and what we do with our training. Yet many people remain fuzzy as to what discipline really means.

I heard an athletics coach once say in regard to discipline, *"Do what has to be done, when it has to be done, as well as it can be done, and do it that way every time."* This is a good definition of discipline for Zen Guitar. Consider each part:

Do what has to be done . . .

In life, there are things we *want* to do and things we know we *should* do. Usually these things conflict. We'd rather spend than save, watch TV instead of study, eat dessert instead of keep to our diet. Discipline is what compels us to follow our higher nature.

When we act out of self-discipline, we feel better about ourselves for having done so. In this way, discipline differs from self-denial. Many people deny themselves things they want in the name of discipline, when they're actually acting out of stubbornness, martyrdom, or fear. Those who act out of self-denial feel no better for having done so. The right thing done in the wrong spirit will manifest itself in other problems on the path of Zen Guitar.

If you have to ask what *has* to be done:

Don't ask, practice.

when it has to be done . . .

The time is now.

When you catch yourself thinking, "I've got to get around to fixing that thing," get out the tools and fix it.

When you hear yourself saying, "I've been meaning to write that letter," sit down and write it.

When you feel that you have so much to do you don't know where to begin, start with one task, however small, and get it done. Then proceed to another. As the samurai say, "Attack the corners"—the little things that stick out—then work your way in to the big things.

A famous zen teaching illustrates the attitude required for this kind of discipline:

A monk approached the zen master Joshu and said, "I have just entered the monastery. Please teach me."

Joshu said, "Have you eaten your rice porridge?"

The monk replied that he had.

"Then you had better wash your bowl," Joshu said.

I saw a similar lesson in discipline at a karate dojo I once visited. The master emerged from his office and signaled a student to turn on the lights to begin class. As the lights came on, one of the bulbs flashed and burned out.

The master proceeded to teach for an hour and a half. When the lesson was over, he walked straight back to his office and emerged with a new light bulb.

There was a man who knew what to do when.

as well as it can be done . . .

If you are going to do something, take care to do it right. There is no sense in practicing half heartedly.

The zen master Banzan was said to have realized this point when, as a youth, he overheard an exchange between a butcher and a customer.

"Give me the best piece of meat you have," the customer said.

"Everything in my shop is the best," the butcher replied. "You cannot find here any piece of meat that is not the best."

The butcher knew he had done his work as well as it could be done.

To truly understand this point of discipline, you must also understand the previous point: when it has to be done. Many times we fail to leave ourselves enough time to do things properly. We either procrastinate or underestimate the time needed to do the job right. If you're going to do something as well as it can be done, give yourself plenty of time. High quality does not come of haste.

and do it that way every time.

The mark of true discipline lies in its consistent application. Surely there were times when the monk had other things to do than wash the dishes, or when the butcher felt too tired to ensure that every cut of meat was the best. How could they sustain such discipline?

The key is not to think of doing things right *every* time; the thought seems too overwhelming. Just do it right one time: *this* time, right now. That's all you ever have to worry about.

Do what has to be done, when it has to be done, as well as it can be done, and do it that way every time. Follow that single rule and you are sure to know the Way of Zen Guitar.

Limits

Approach [your] guitar intelligently, and if there are limits, don't deny them. Work within your restrictions. Some things you can do better than others, some things you can't do as well. So accentuate the positive.

—Chet Atkins

It is said that trees do not grow to the sky. Human beings are like this, too. All of us have limited physical capacities. No matter how much we train, some weights are simply too heavy to lift, some heights too high to scale, some spaces too small to fit. Try as we might to perfect a certain skill, it can remain beyond our ability.

Those who follow the path of Zen Guitar must eventually confront their personal limits. What's required is to test these limits, push them, and finally, to know them and accept them.

Once we understand our limits, we can begin to work around them. Oftentimes, limits lead us to creative alternatives we would never have discovered otherwise. For example, a Japanese pianist I know had hands so small she couldn't make the stretch necessary to play certain classical pieces. She began writing her own pieces to take account of her limited hand width, and became a respected composer.

We find our limits by taking on challenges. If a teacher gives you an assignment you think is too easy, do a little more than is asked—not out of ego, to show how smart you are, or to gain favor, but out of a sincere desire for self-improvement. Pace yourself, but push to find your own limit.

If a teacher gives you an assignment you think is too difficult, make every effort to complete it. The teacher may know your limits better than you do.

Some limits we simply can't work around. Once acquired, knowledge of these limits can be painful, shattering our dreams and aspirations. But the Way of Zen Guitar is to know reality, to accept what is. We cannot dwell on the unattainable. Some things are simply not in our destiny.

When we start out in the world, each of us is handed a seed. None of us knows what that seed will become, but we must nurture it, help it grow, and accept its nature. If it turns out to be a lemon tree, then, as the saying goes, learn to make lemonade. As a corollary I'd add: Make it as well as you can, and love doing it.

If you find contentment in the talent you've been given, you'll have no need for envy. Some people have all the talent in the world and never find happiness, while others of modest ability live totally at peace with themselves. Who do you think is further on the path of Zen Guitar?

I do not mean that one should become complacent on the path; no one ever discovers every limit. The quest to always learn more about one's art deepens its very mystery. Those who say, "I have no need to learn music theory," or "I don't ever care to learn a diminished chord," are really just shutting themselves off from learning. One new insight or one new chord can open a whole new world.

Know what works best for you; above all else, you must be natural. But always be of the mind to learn.

Remember, even though trees do not grow to the sky, their roots continue to grow. You've been given all you need to know the Way of Zen Guitar without looking to anyone or anyplace else. Just keep digging where you are.

Follow-Through

I don't think of myself as a symbol of the Sixties, but I do think of myself as a symbol—of following through on your beliefs.

——Joan Baez

The path of Zen Guitar is never ending. But short-term goals can focus the mind so long as one takes care to stay on the path. Whatever goals you set—playing a solo mistake free, landing a gig, recording an album—should not be viewed as ends unto themselves, but as points along the path. Follow through in everything you do—the road goes on forever.

A Chinese proverb says, "In a hundred-mile march, ninety is about the halfway point." Without the proper follow-through, all that preceded can be lost. Life experience bears this out in small and large ways. Victory on the battlefield can be rendered meaningless by one flaw in the peace agreement. A 300-yard tee shot in golf will mean little if one misses a three-foot putt. A figure skater's whole routine collapses with a fall on the last jump. That new recording you perfected in the studio goes for naught with careless mastering at the record plant.

It's human nature to anticipate the finish—attainment of the goal. But in so doing, we can easily lose track of the present moment and the task at hand. Like the sprinter in a 100-meter race, carry the spirit of running *through* the finish line. Do not focus on the goal; focus only on the process by which you arrive at the goal. When you find yourself imagining what will be, remember: Nothing happens until it happens.

隙

Suki

Even in single tasks—stroking a tennis ball, shooting a basketball, strumming a chord—your spirit must follow through to the other side of the moment. Failure to follow through cuts your spirit short. Zen masters call this failure *suki*: "stopping mind." At all times, you want your mind to flow smoothly without hesitation.

I once heard a Japanese flute player say that during practice his teacher would walk off into the next room and attend to other tasks. Upon returning, the teacher would say, "When I didn't notice your playing, it was good. When I did notice it, it was bad." What the teacher noticed was the student's suki. When the student played flowingly, the teacher became lost in his tasks. But when the student hesitated, the teacher lost his own flow of thinking and became *aware* of hearing the music.

If, in the spirit of a true unsui, your thoughts float like the clouds and flow like water, you will avoid suki. A cloud or river never stops moving; it continues on and on. Follow through in every aspect of your training, then follow through some more.

Taste

*Not everyone is going to like what I do, and that's something
I can accept; if everyone liked what I did, I probably wouldn't be
playing anything of depth.*

———Joshua Redman

No matter how well you play, no matter how large your spirit, no matter how much your sound speaks the truth, some people simply will not be moved. Your music will not appeal to their taste.

All of us in this world have our individual tastes; that's what gives life its spice. Some people like their food salty, others like it peppery, others like it sweet, and others like it sour. This goes for music as well. Harmonies that sound angelic to one person may sound too saccharin to another. Chord changes that sound profound to someone sitting in Row 8 may sound too arty to a listener in Row 9.

Some players make commercial calculations and compromise their taste in an effort to appeal to a wider audience, yet they still run the risk of rejection. If it winds up that player and listener alike don't like the music, what is the point of playing?

Do not mistake me: I believe in such a thing as good taste and poor taste. A guitar player must have aesthetic principles. But my judgments will not be the same as yours.

On the path of Zen Guitar, develop your sense of taste as you would your sense of hearing. Learn from those players whose taste you like. Then trust your taste like the cook who knows how hot he likes his chili. If rejection follows, so be it. At least you have satisfied yourself.

Remember, too, that tastes can change. Some music we learn to appreciate with study. Some music grows on us with the passage of time. And some music we ignore for years until it catches us at exactly the right moment as we are driving down the highway.

Play the truth and it will remain the truth for listeners to discover when they are ready.

Collaboration

You can't compute or calculate the chemistry that arises when you put together a band. . . . No one knows until you start working together.

—Jimmy Page

Each of us walks our own path in this dojo. But we often find the Way of Zen Guitar through collaboration.

Those who study here must learn how to play together with others—to participate in a group effort, to lean on someone and be leaned on, to subjugate one's ego for the good of the group. These lessons apply to every social relationship. As a jazz player once said, all true musicians can get along; it's people who can't get along. Always endeavor to find the way of harmony and you'll stay on the path of Zen Guitar.

Through collaborating with others, we learn to align our hyoshi, our natural rhythm, with the hyoshi of those around us. Therein we establish a groove.

When you start to work with someone, keep three things in mind: company, vision, and chemistry.

Company
Surround yourself with good people in every endeavor. Work with those who are professional, competent, committed to excellence, and passionate about what they do; you can learn from them and your work will benefit.

Beware of people who would build their own ego by cutting you down. Beware, too, of sycophants who would build your ego to preserve their mediocrity. Both types care more about their position in life than their work.

When someone in your company is unprofessional, incompetent, or indifferent, you are the one who suffers.

Vision

When your collaborator has a strong vision of where to go and you do not, follow the vision.

When you have a strong vision of where to go and your collaborators do not, invite them along and help them see it.

If no one in the project has a strong vision of where to go, develop a common vision before you start working, or at minimum find one before you finish. A project with no vision yields mediocre results at best, and usually wastes everyone's time.

When more than one strong vision exists and they conflict, work to find a consensus. Know when conflict arises from true artistic differences and when it stems from ego. If you put the partnership first, you will sacrifice for the good of the whole. But do nothing to dilute the strength of the final vision. To paraphrase an old adage, too many producers in the studio spoil the mix.

Chemistry

With most groups in life, we don't bond. With a few groups, we do. On those rare occasions, learn what it means to band and *be* a band.

A band is not merely a collection of individuals. Its essential character must be for the whole to exceed the sum of the parts. When the right people get together, be it in music or sports or business or marriage or sex or whatever, a kind of spiritual fusion takes place. This fusion cannot be bought or forced or manufactured. It simply happens from the chemistry of nature.

Most groups of people have no chemistry. Like a random collection of molecules, they don't combine to make anything special. Their particular level of talent makes no difference. Examples abound in the music world of supergroups and all-star jams that fail to produce inspiring music.

Every now and then, though, two hydrogen molecules will collide with one molecule of oxygen. The resulting mix takes on a character far beyond its basic elements. So it is with human beings as well. This chemistry defines a great band.

Human chemistry is not a science. No one knows how this magic happens. But when it does, we feel the presence of something divine, and everyone who's there knows it. Cherish the chemistry of great bands wherever you find it. You're onto something big.

The Twelve Common Missteps

Self-Doubt
Instant Gratification
Ego
Halfheartedness
Overearnestness
Speed
Competition
Obsession
Mishandled Criticism
Failure to Adjust
Loss of Focus
Overthinking

Self-Doubt

I like to play with people who can play simple and are not threatened by other musicians thinking they can't play. And that eliminates 99 percent of the musicians.

—Neil Young

For long stretches of the path, there will be periods of self-doubt. You may hear others making beautiful music and wonder if you can ever do the same. Rest assured, you can—but you must maintain perspective.

The Way of Zen Guitar is to play what you are *meant* to play, not necessarily what you *want* to play. Understand the difference. Sometimes the two are the same, sometimes they are not. You must reconcile one with the other or you will not make any progress on the path.

All you can ever do here is be yourself and play your song. If you ask, "But will it be good enough to play Carnegie Hall or the Village Vanguard or Budokan?" you are blind to the Way. A bird does not ask, "Is my song pretty?" Just make a joyful noise.

One can play the greatest stages in the world and still be spiritually adrift; talent alone does not bring inner peace. If you work to find peace within yourself, you will have no self-doubt about your music, your talent, or anything else.

The feeling of self-doubt means you have lost your beginner's mind. You must regain the sense of starting over. Trust in the truth of naive musicianship; there you will find what you are meant to play.

Naive musicianship is exactly as the name implies: innocent, unself-conscious, egoless expression. It follows no rules other than its own, and seeks acceptance on nothing but its own terms. It flows out of the African proverb that says: "If you can talk you can sing, if you can walk you can dance."

Play what you can that sounds good to your ear. Don't concern yourself with whether people will like it. Be as the child who makes up an innocent melody. The most primitive music, played simply with maximum emotion, can be profound. So long as the spirit is pure, the music will be too. It takes so little to make good music—three chords can do it.

Look at the way some people whip up a fine meal using whatever is left in the refrigerator, or watch the way a toddler makes a toy out of a piece of trash. It's a process of pure creative imagination, using whatever means are available.

With a beginner's mind you can lose your bearings and let your openness lead you to new ones. Study what your ears tell you and learn from everything you hear. If you make a mistake, take note. Oftentimes you can use it to hear in a new way—to discover the unexpected. Let these accidents be a key to creation. Instead of learning how to do something and then doing it, *do something* and then learn from what you did. Rediscover the joy of beginning and your doubt will vanish.

Never forget: The Way of Zen Guitar is within you. You must discover the key to unlock it.

Instant Gratification

The general attitude is, "I want it, and I want it now!" But it
really takes years if you're going to do it right, and a lot of kids
just don't want to take the time to work on it and see where it's
all going, and what it means, and where it comes from, and how
they should apply it and use it in playing their songs. It doesn't
make any difference how technically good you are or fast you are
or how many notes you know; you just can't do it in two years.

——Johnny Winter

Some people are never satisfied with their rate of progress on the path of Zen Guitar. They believe if they train twice as hard, they can halve the time it takes for them to earn a black belt. This is like thinking, "If I stay awake twice as long, I can live a year's time in six months." Progress on the path of Zen Guitar will not come at any rate other than is natural. You can't live a year in anything but a year's time.

Too many of us today want instant gratification. Some schools feed into this syndrome. I have seen advertisements for programs that promise, "Learn to play guitar in just 24 hours!" We want reward without work. We want the thinking done for us. We want to understand something right away or we can't be bothered. This attitude demeans the accomplishments of those who are true masters.

Only the fetus in the womb has all its needs satisfied as soon as it wants. Too many people seem stuck in this kind of infantilism. Maturity means learning the value of that which is hard-earned. Do not think you'll learn something in this dojo without effort.

The Way of Zen Guitar will never come to those who want it easily. It cannot be purchased or copied or stolen. It can only be known the way a seed grows into a tree—through the passage of time. You have just now planted your seed. Let it grow.

Ego

If I can get out of the way, if I can be pure enough, if I can be selfless enough, and if I can be generous and loving and caring enough to abandon what I have and my own preconceived, silly notions of what I think I am—and become truly who in fact I am, which is really just another child of God—then the music can really use me. And therein lies my fulfillment. That's when the music starts to happen.

—John McLaughlin

You must have enough ego to have a strong sense of self. But too much ego will lead you off the path.

The world today is full of people who lack a healthy ego balance. It has become fashionable to talk trash, to speak boastfully of oneself or disparage the efforts of another. Guitar players, as a class, are not excepted. There is a macho attitude that infects much of the guitar world, where players sport a gunslinger mentality—swaggering in their talent. The attitude is akin to people flaunting the fact they have a black belt so as to intimidate others. All of this stems from an ego that feels so small it must inflate itself through public attention.

This may work as a psychological ploy in competition, but music is not a competition. In this school, those who would think to flaunt their belt level have far to go in their training.

Another form of egoism is false modesty. It is insincerity that stems from an overly large ego. The players secure in themselves and sure of their ability have no need to pump up or play down their egos or puncture the egos around them. They know who they are and what they can do. That is enough.

Ego really leads players astray when they begin to pursue fame as an end unto itself. Music becomes a mere means to acquiring money, status, or adulation. To them, the music doesn't matter, so long as it sells and brings attention.

In this dojo, the integrity of the music comes first. One should strive to make sound with the purity of a bird in the wild—that is the Way of Zen Guitar.

Those people whose ambition is the acquisition of fame or money may work hard to get where they are and what they have. But the world is full of rich and famous people who feel empty inside. The Way of Zen Guitar is through spiritual riches, not material riches. In the end, power and money are like footprints on the beach compared to the Way—here one moment and then washed away. Those who think themselves to be the center of the universe fail to see the truth: It is they who house the universe, not the other way around.

A final word of caution: Never underestimate the potential of ego to lead one astray, no matter how hard you train or what your point on the path. The rush of learning a new skill, the flattery that accompanies a touch of success—these things can overinflate any person's ego. Too much praise can do damage just like too much criticism. Measure a compliment the same as you measure a critique. If you think you've arrived some-where, you've got that much farther to go.

One can lose the Way in an instant.

Halfheartedness

If [you're] going to sweep the floor, sweep it better than anybody in town. And if you're going to play the guitar, really, really, really get in it, and don't be jivin'.

—Carlos Santana

Do not trudge along your path. Your spirit shows in every step.

So many of the things we do in life, we do halfheartedly. In the classroom, on the job, at the dinner table, we can show up and not be all there. If you find your feet dragging, check your path. You're probably on the wrong one.

To move down the path of Zen Guitar, you must commit your heart to training. The only way to do this is to love it. If guitar playing isn't fun for you, then something is seriously wrong. All the effort you put in should only increase your joy.

To check the spirit of those who seem halfhearted, I send them to the blackboard. In schools of old, teachers would punish students by requiring them to write the same phrase repeatedly on the blackboard—"I will not talk in class" and such. In the Zen Guitar Dojo, students go to the blackboard not out of punishment, but for training.

Somewhere in you, there are words you can get behind with your whole heart and soul—words that say, "This is who I am, and this is what I believe." They may be as simple as, "I am

here." Or they may be more philosophical: "The only opponent is within." Whatever the words, you must find them in
yourself and write them on the blackboard 10,000 times. To do
so, you must mean it with your whole heart.

What you say can put you right back on the path.

Overearnestness

Take it easy, but take it.

——Woody Guthrie

The opposite of halfheartedness is overearnestness. You must pursue the Way of Zen Guitar sincerely, but don't try too hard.

Some guitarists are simply too eager to please. Like people who overpursue a romantic relationship, they push themselves on an audience without allowing the listener any space to come to them. Even if these players make a positive first impression, in short order we start to lose respect for them.

Other guitarists are prone to going "over the top" with excesses of emotion or pyrotechnics. Like people who enthusiastically start a new workout routine and then injure themselves, these players don't know how to pace themselves. Their spirit is like beer pouring too fast into a glass, foaming over without control. They've yet to learn how to fill the glass exactly to the brim.

One indicator of overearnestness is playing at too high a volume. Without question, some music sounds best when played loud. But many players mistakenly equate volume with passion and intensity. The feeling is akin to someone speaking loudly at a foreigner, as if volume alone will aid in comprehension.

Playing at high volume means taking all the current in a room and harnessing it, like a jockey controlling a racehorse.

In the hands of a novice, a loud guitar feeds back wildly, like a colt being guided by an inexperienced rider. With time, though, we learn to control a loud guitar the way a veteran horseman handles the reins of a steed. Although we feel the power, a measure of restraint shows through.

Study hard, but stay relaxed. You never want the feeling of pressing; instead, learn the feeling of power held in reserve. If your spirit is too strong, you have yet to master yourself. The measure of mastery is not through what you show, but what you hold back. Self-control is the key.

Apply this thinking to your playing and your life. The Way is through restraint.

Speed

My chops were not as fast . . . [but] I just leaned more on what was in my mind than what was in my chops. I learned a long time ago that one note can go a long way if it's the right one, and it will probably whip the guy with twenty notes.

——Les Paul

Too many players, young ones in particular, become obsessed with playing fast, thinking speed is the measure of ability; the faster the fingers, they believe, the better the player. This shows their immaturity.

Music is not a race. One does not gain points for sticking more notes into a solo than the next person. Speed is a byproduct of technique—not an end to be pursued in itself. It means nothing apart from the context of the music. It is far more important for a musician to understand tempo, timing, pacing, and quickness. Focus on these dynamics and you will begin to know hyoshi, the feeling of natural rhythm.

Tempo

Every song proceeds at a certain rate of speed, like a car on the road. Play too fast and the song feels rushed, as though given too much gas. Play too slow and the tune wobbles like the wheels coming off an axle. The right speed feels like a well-built car taking a corner with the driver in full control. Know that feeling in your music and you will understand tempo.

Pacing

How you play within the tempo—that is pacing. Against a slow tempo, a certain guitar run may sound fast, while against a fast tempo, the same run would sound slow. Learn to think like the baseball pitcher who gets hitters out by changing speeds. After a series of slow pitches, a fastball looks that much faster. Know when to speed up and when to slow down. These are the dynamics of pacing.

Timing

Timing is having a sense of the moment—a feel for exactly when to strike. The punchline delivered a moment too soon or a moment too late can kill a joke's impact. So it is with notes in music. The difference between the exact right moment and the wrong moment can be the breadth of a baby's eyelash. Understand this and you will understand timing.

Quickness

If anything, Zen Guitar prizes quickness over speed. Quickness is the speed of thought to action. It demands control; there is no feeling of haste in quickness. How often in conversation have we said after a verbal exchange, "What I should have said was . . ." It is the same in playing the guitar. When we're quick, thought and action happen simultaneously.

If you play what the music calls for, you will never have to worry about your speed. The matter will take care of itself.

Competition

*Differences of opinion . . . [are] part of collaborating with
another human being. But music is not a competitive thing.
I don't want to deal with someone who's in competition with me,
I want to work together and make music.*

——Edward Van Halen

M any people need to infuse their activity with an element of competition in order to motivate themselves.
Even in an exercise club where the training is solitary, machines
like the Stairmaster, stationary bike, and treadmill have a "race"
feature built in that allows users to compete against the machine. For many people, this mentality carries over into music.
From "Battle of the Bands" shows to the one-upmanship of
jazz "cutting contests" to winning a spot in the orchestra pit on
Broadway, the music world—like the world at large—is rife
with competition.

When it is healthy, competition serves a useful purpose. Jazz
players adhere to the axiom that "competition can produce rev-
elations." By pitting our skills against another person's, we
learn about ourselves—how far we can go, how we respond to
pressure, where we need to improve.

But oftentimes in music, competitive attitudes create disharmony. Instead of being put to constructive use, competition
brings out a player's insecurity. Many players use competition

not as a means to test themselves, but to *prove* themselves. Should you feel such a need, check your ego. What are you trying to prove, and why?

The Way of Zen Guitar is not a competition. Those who train here should measure themselves first against their own standards and capabilities. We all have a song we are meant to play born inside of us. To put these songs in competition with each other would be like pitting a child's fingerpainting against a work of French impressionism. Each must be judged on its own merits.

I do not dispute the fact of talent; some people seem born with a genius for music while others struggle and struggle. But no matter what we do in life, there will always be people with more talent in some regard, just as there will always be people with less. We must learn to accept our place with humility and grace, not smugness or jealousy. Witnessing true genius should inspire us to find our own path in life, not discourage us because we can't follow someone else's.

Golfers like to say they do not compete against each other, they compete against the course. Zen Guitar is like that. If you must inject competition into your training, channel it inward. Resolve never to be outdone in the Way of Zen Guitar.

The only opponent is within.

Obsession

For me, I think the only danger is being too much in love with guitar playing. The music *is the most important thing, and the guitar is only the instrument.*

—————Jerry Garcia

Some schools teach that you must think, breathe, and live guitar twenty-four hours a day. This is obsessive. In this school, you must think, breathe, and live, *then* play guitar.

"From one thing, know ten thousand things" means to extrapolate from the specific to the universal—to see the broad truth in a single action. The golfer who sees the tree only as an obstacle, the sand only as a trap, and the water only as a hazard may be a skilled technician, but will never reach the level of artistry.

If all you know is the guitar to the exclusion of everything else, your playing will be empty. You must relate your guitar playing to the world at large, and vice versa. Study the brief bloom of the cherry blossom in spring. Hear the music in the way the breeze blows its petals gently to the ground. Feel how every petal lets go only when it is ready. You can find the Way of Zen Guitar through this.

What you bring to your playing is the sum of what you are.

Mishandled Criticism

I saw [Bob] Dylan getting criticized in Australia by this guy who was saying, "Your new songs aren't as relevant as your old songs." And Dylan just said, "Well, I'm out here writing songs—what are you doing?"

——Tom Petty

The student of Zen Guitar needs to know but two things about criticism: how to give it and how to take it.

If you must criticize, do so in the spirit of building up, not tearing down. Tearing down is easy. The Way of Zen Guitar is to build. This is extremely difficult.

When receiving criticism, learn from that which is given in the spirit of building. Ignore that which attempts to tear down; do not allow anything to pierce your armor. Critics can be quick to find fault with an idea, but empty when it comes to providing an alternative.

No matter what you do or how respected you are, you can't please everyone. Learn to recognize the different kinds of critics:

Those people whose criticism stems from a difference in taste. Just because someone's taste is different doesn't mean it's better.

Those who criticize in hindsight without understanding the circumstances of the moment. It's easy to play Monday-morning quarterback and quite a different matter to be on the field facing the blitz.

Those whose criticism stems from ego—that is, a desire to show how clever they are, or a feeling of insecurity. Through cutting others they seek to make themselves look better.

Use your training here to become your own best critic. Then no one can tell you what you don't already know.

A final word on self-criticism: Do not beat up on yourself. Even if you think you know your flaws, there is no need to advertise them. Most people won't have noticed.

Failure to Adjust

Things turn out better by accident sometimes. But you can't organize accidents.

——Jeff Beck

There is a lot of randomness in the world. A guitar string breaks in midperformance. A fuse blows in the amplifier. Rain falls on an open-air gig. Try as we might to control the variables in our lives, things happen moment to moment that force us to adjust to changing circumstances. In such cases, learn to see the glass as half full, not half empty, and make the best of the situation.

The Japanese word for crisis, *kiki*, translates two ways: as "danger occasion," but also "danger opportunity." Look for the opportunity in the chance occurrence. How you react to the unexpected reveals your true spirit. In this dojo, learn to fall like a cat—on your feet.

危機

Kiki

I once saw a gig where the band's sound system blew out in the middle of their biggest song. The guitars and vocals went completely dead; only the live drums made a sound.

Without stopping, the band finished the number by leading the audience in a giant sing-along.

After that, the sound system returned. But that one song remained the defining moment of the show: When things fell apart, the band made art.

Sometimes we're lucky, sometimes we're not. Then again, luck can be a matter of attitude.

Loss of Focus

I remember coming to a concert where they had a big catered meal set out for everyone. . . . I went and said, "Miles, man, you gotta see all this food they got here." And Miles said, "I didn't come here to eat."

—Gary Bartz, recalling a conversation with Miles Davis

In Japan there is a saying, "You can't chase two rabbits at once." It reminds us to avoid distraction and stay on course. So often we lose focus and start running willy-nilly between rabbits instead of making sure we catch just one.

Whenever we lose our point of focus, we can usually blame either a lack of concentration or a lack of commitment.

Lack of concentration

In a world of sound bites, quick cuts, and channel surfing, it becomes harder and harder to sustain a complex thought or task. The Way of Zen Guitar is to fight the short attention span.

An exercise that zen masters use to develop concentration instructs students to sit silently and count slowly from one to ten in their minds. If anything should interrupt their count—self-consciousness, a stray thought, awareness of hearing a noise, or even the sound of their own breathing—they must start over from one.

Try this exercise the next time you lose focus. If you can count past one, you will not lack for concentration.

If you can make it to ten, you will know the Way of Zen Guitar.

Lack of commitment

Problems with concentration often result from a lack of commitment. Today we see many people jumping from job to job and relationship to relationship, starting projects and never following through, because they can't commit to anything. They wander through life looking for a better path rather than polishing their own.

When we look around at what other people have and where they are going, we lose focus on what's important: what *we* have and where *we* are going.

Yes, there is more than one path to the top of the mountain. But the only one that will get you there is your own. Do not look longingly at the paths of others. Give yours your undivided attention and keep your focus. The farther you go on your own path, the more you will understand every other path.

At the end, they all converge.

Overthinking

I don't think about the meaning of it all. I say, just plug in your damn guitar and make some noise.
                              ——Paul Westerberg, The Replacements

Do not analyze things to death. Sometimes the best strategy is, "Ready, fire, aim." Do it first, then make adjustments. The answer lies in action—not in words.   ○

Kuro: Black

responsibility

Some people have a great sense of moral responsibility; unfortunately, it's backed up with a poor sense of musical taste. Other people have great musical ability, and very little sense of moral responsibility. It's very difficult to have a good balance.

—Eric Clapton

Those who train hard enough and long enough get to a point where body, mind, and spirit come into balance. The body has developed its own intelligence and the mind trusts this intelligence, allowing the spirit to express itself. One's playing becomes so fluid, thought and action seem to occur simultaneously.

To reach this point on the path of Zen Guitar, you must be good at what you do. But to truly know the Way, it's not enough to be good at what you do. You must go beyond.

One does not earn the black belt through technical proficiency alone. In this school, even the most dazzling guitar skills are not enough to turn the belt black. There may be players with monstrous chops, who know every kind of style, whose playing can whip an audience into a frenzy or drop a listener's jaw. But if they lack the proper character, their belt is not black in this dojo.

The Way of Zen Guitar requires responsibility and truly giving of one's self. Only through accepting our debt to the world and giving something back does our song have any meaning.

The Japanese language is again instructive here. The very word for human being, *ningen*, suggests a connection to the surrounding world. *Nin* means person, while *gen* means "space." In other words, we only become human—a *ningen*—in relation to the space around us.

Ningen

To live responsibly means to be accountable for ourselves, our actions, and our charges. Many people today refuse to accept this. From child neglect to juvenile misconduct, even to murder, we see people looking to shift blame from themselves, pretend innocence, or walk away from a mess of their own making. There are musicians who, in the name of artistic freedom, espouse violence, racial hatred, and sexism, then disavow the ripple effects of their actions. Many more exploit the media to gain fame, yet refuse to accept that they serve as role models for young people.

This is not the Way of Zen Guitar. Those who wish to earn the black belt here should accept, at minimum, five responsibilities:

A responsibility to yourself
Apply yourself and develop your talent to the fullest capacity, without excuses.

A responsibility to your talent
Put your talent to good use, not to bad, in the service of something outside yourself, and do nothing to waste it.

A responsibility to your art
Express your song truthfully, in the face of all opposition.

A responsibility to your audience
Respect those who come to you with open ears and foster a sense of community.

A responsibility to the Way
Act as sensei to those who sincerely seek to find their own path, and share with them what you know to be true. The Way is for everyone.

To abdicate even one responsibility is to diverge from the path of Zen Guitar.

Giving of ourselves—sharing a song purely—does not mean we need to perform in front of crowds; one can share a song sitting alone in a forest, so long as the spirit is right. To share a song purely, it must arise from the soul without thought or regard to getting something back. Training to do this takes the deepest kind of soul searching. We haven't gone far enough until we come face-to-face with the very principles by which we live our lives—what we believe and how we treat others.

In this dojo, the purest song is the one shared through humility, openness, and generosity. We learn these qualities here as we work to develop our chops; the process is one and the same.

Through the frustrations of learning a new skill, we learn humility—how much we don't know.

Through the exploration of knowledge, we learn openness—a willingness to try new things, to see things from another person's perspective.

Through playing with others, we learn generosity—how to share and contribute to the good of the group.

The path to a black belt is not through becoming the best player, but the best person. Raise your *living* to the level of an art form, and your playing will reflect it. That is the Way of Zen Guitar.

In this section, I have divided the teachings into three categories:

Black-Belt Head describes the mind of the Zen Guitarist at this stage of the path—the thinking, strategies, and knowledge used to follow the Way.

Black-Belt Hand covers the physical aspects of playing at this level—the posture, touch, and feelings that characterize an advanced understanding of Zen Guitar.

Black-Belt Heart concerns the spirit of high-level Zen Guitar—the attitude, awareness, and devotion required of those who come this far.

Through these teachings, you will learn what characterizes excellence in this dojo—and what does not.

Black Belt Head

Know One Thing
Make a Statement
Decide
Prepare the Mind
Establish the Context
Play the Changes
Draw the Frame
Zoom In, Zoom Out
Trust the Tale
Attend to Detail
Thought: Process

Know One Thing

Writer to Frank Zappa: *Have there been parts of your life that you've neglected because you've been absorbed in your music?*

Zappa: *Well what am I missing? Do I regret not going horseback riding, or learning how to water ski? Well, no. I don't want to climb mountains, I don't want to do bungie-jumping. I haven't missed any of these things. If you're absorbed by some-*thing, *what's to miss?*

Many people hear the phrase "black-belt Zen Guitarist" and think it means a thorough proficiency in all aspects of guitar playing. This is not necessarily the case.

To be sure, there are black-belt players who know the guitar inside and out, the same way there are chefs who can prepare a different delicacy seven nights a week. But others may know only one song, like the grandmother who cooks only one meal each Sunday—her special lasagna, with a secret recipe that will get handed down from generation to generation. The grandmother may not have the talent and range of the star chef, but both are black belts in their own way.

In other words, to be a black belt in this dojo, all you need to know is one thing: where your passion lies. If you follow that passion to find the truth for your life, your belt will be black in Zen Guitar.

For some people, "one thing" may be playing the guitar or singing a particular song. For others it could be sailing or hiking or child rearing. Whatever the case, knowing that one thing gives our life meaning and makes it worth getting up in the morning.

Endeavoring to know one thing does not mean becoming a specialist to the exclusion of all other knowledge. In fact, too many specialists burrow themselves in their corner of learning without connecting what they do to the world at large.

In this dojo, knowing one thing means to see the relationship of what we do to everything around us. If your passion is simply to play one song, study the spirit and character of that song until you know what unites it with all the other songs of the world. Through one song, or even one note, you can find the true meaning of harmony.

On the other hand, you may view your "one thing" more broadly. There are athletes in track and field, for example, who don't excel at the high jump, sprinting, or the pole vault, but thrive in the decathlon. Maybe you're not the best guitar player on your block, but your collective passions—for music, your family, your friends—make you a black belt in life.

The Way of Zen Guitar is to know the depth of one thing, however large or small, and from that one thing, to know ten thousand things. Get to the bottom of your song, and you will know what you need to know. That is all.

Make a Statement

The question is, "What are you saying with [the guitar]?" Not "Can you play this lick?" or "What's your speed like?" It's, "What are you saying with your instrument? What is being communicated in this song?"

——The Edge, U2

A teacher of mine once walked into an instrument dealership and began testing a guitar with an eye toward buying it.

After a time, the salesman said, "You know, you're the first person to come in here all day who's played a *song*."

The vast majority of people, when handed a guitar, simply noodle—that is, their fingers run up and down the guitar playing notes and phrases that form no coherent statement. It is the musical equivalent of babbling at the mouth. Even within the context of performance, many players let their fingers fly without thought, running off a flurry of notes, grabbing the whammy bar, bathing themselves in feedback. They seem to be saying something, but the notes go in one ear and out the other without adding up to anything. They lack a coherent concept.

Think of all the guitar solos you hear in popular music. How many of them are transcendent or truly memorable? This is not to say these players lack impressive technique. It merely suggests their playing veers toward self-indulgence—a kind of musical masturbation.

The Way of Zen Guitar is not through self-indulgence, but self-awareness. Everything you play says something about you—how you think, what you think, the way you view yourself and your art. Know why you play, and make it stand for something. You should not regard your music as disposable any more than you would regard yourself as such.

You do not need lyrics to make a statement, either. Words can crystallize your message, but the music carries a message of its own. A good beat or a pretty melody can make a song work *in spite* of insipid lyrics; it's much harder to work the other way around. Like the sound of laughter or a lover's nibble on the ear, Zen Guitar should communicate heart to heart, soul to soul, without any filter from the mind.

Self-indulgence is when a player feels the music without caring whether or not the listener does. The black belt here knows what it means to put an idea across—to give something to the listener with character, content, and concision.

Character

To make a statement with character means delivering an honest, uncompromising vision that stays true to itself and succeeds or fails on its own terms. It may be a furious jazz solo over complex changes, or one note sustained over a three-chord blues. Complexity does not matter. What counts is your honesty and integrity.

Content

Content means the depth of feeling one puts into each note—the emotional resonance of the statement. Masters of the Japanese tea ceremony use the term *kokoro ire*: inclusion of the heart's spirit.

Kokoro ire

Like sobbing or excitement or anger, the emotions of music bridge all cultural boundaries, transcending language and the need for intellectual understanding. I have seen Japanese youths thrusting their fists in the air, singing American rock anthems while not comprehending a single word. What they hear is the kokoro ire. The emotional content of the song is what makes it resonate across cultures.

Concision

Concision means to say what you have to say economically, in the fewest notes possible. Make the statement only as long as it needs to be, with nothing wasted. Do not stray from the point. That does not mean you need to keep all solos short. You can write a three-hour symphony if that's the length needed to convey your vision. But what you say should take no longer than is necessary.

Life is a process of learning to live with limits—limited resources, the limited attention spans of listeners, our limited time on this earth. Learn to pack the most into the least. Know the mind of the haiku poet who has but three lines and seventeen syllables with which to work. There is a reason these poets often write of the cherry blossom with its brief, brilliant bloom.

I know there are people in this world who enjoy excess, the kind who judge restaurants by the generosity of the portions. But to me, putting too much food on the plate is wasteful and unappetizing. A good chef delivers exactly the right portion so that the plate comes back with every bite eaten and the diner neither overstuffed nor underserved.

Music is the same way. Pare away excess until you're left with the perfect serving. This demands a deep understanding of phrasing, tone, timing, rhythm—all those things that enable you to say something just so. If three notes will suffice instead of four, play three. Do not waste a single moment. It is bad enough to waste your own time; show utmost respect for the listener's.

If anything, err on the side of economy. Leave the listeners wanting more; they can always ask for an encore.

Decide

If it does right by the song, you've made the right choice.
—Robbie Robertson

To paraphrase the words of a learned man, guitar players are people who make things. What they make fore-most—what determines their artistry—is decisions.

I have said before that anything you set out to make, make as well as you can. Play *decisively*. Know when to play and what to play, and conversely, when not to play and what not to play.

To achieve this kind of clarity, the black-belt player must train so hard as to obviate the very need for decisions. One of zen's most famous riddles frames the challenge like this:

Imagine yourself hanging by your teeth from a tree over a cliff. Your hands can grab no branch, your feet can touch no limb. A man from below asks you a question your life depends on answering. You cannot remain silent, yet if you open your mouth, you fall to your death. What do you do?

If you make a decision, you're finished. If you truly know the Way of Zen Guitar, your song will answer for you.

Prepare the Mind

I try to be prepared for the moment, through understanding and being warmed up, knowing all about chords and scales, so I don't even have to think and I can get right to what it is I want to say.
———Pat Metheny

The best way to make decisions about playing in the moment is to have already made them. That is, do your thinking ahead of time. Think before the time comes to act, think before the time comes to speak, think before the time comes play a note. Then, when the moment arrives, do not think. Just play.

Some athletes prepare themselves by visualizing what they want to do, creating a mental movie of themselves in perfect action. Golfers picture the perfect swing, pole vaulters imagine the perfect jump, figure skaters run through the perfect routine. Musicians who perform a set piece of music can also visualize themselves playing the perfect song. The sharper and more detailed your mind's movie, the more likely your hands will reproduce it.

Players of improvised music can't visualize what they are going to play, because by definition they don't know where the moment will take them. But they can prepare strategies for dealing with the unexpected. The black-belt player's thinking is the same as that of a fielder in baseball. Before every pitch, a good fielder analyzes the game situation and says, "If the ball is hit to me over here, I will make this play. If the ball is hit to me over there, I will make that play." There are countless plays that might develop. When the ball is hit, there is no time to think—training and mental preparation must take over.

So it is with playing music in the moment. With the proper mental attitude and training, what you play should come out as natural as the call of a bird in the wild. There is no thought, not even so much as a word in your head—only the song of the heart. The instant that discrimination and calculation enter the mind, the truth of the moment is lost. To play the truth, you must already have the correct attitude. When you look for it during the moment, you will still be looking for it when the moment has passed.

Establish the Context

You might not feel like playing pretty all the time. Instead, you might want to play something nasty. . . . [Y]ou might want to play something out of context with the tune. It might be a note that creates so much tension it becomes unpleasant, but you want it to sound that way.

—George Benson

Martial artists train for years to learn hundreds of different self-defense techniques. Yet in any given fight, a combatant need rely only upon a few moves.

Those few moves, however, vary from opponent to opponent.

Zen Guitar is the same. At any given gig, you needn't show your whole repertoire. Choose what you use according to the context of the situation. Just as a bow and arrow are good from a distance but useless in close combat, so it is sometimes with certain musical styles, tones, notes, or phrases.

The Way of Zen Guitar is such that it applies at any time, in any situation; the truth assumes ten thousand shapes and forms. But know which truth is operative at each moment. Sometimes the nail that sticks up gets hammered down; other times, the squeaky wheel gets the grease. It depends on the context.

Play the Changes

When the chord changes, you should change.

—Joe Pass

J once spoke to a friend about a tribute concert he saw featuring many different guitarists. One song had a rock guitarist soloing over a jazz number. I asked how that went.

My friend sighed. "He didn't play the changes."

In music, as in life, playing the changes can be difficult. Change takes us out of the known, where we are comfortable, to a place that requires us to find new harmony. Sudden, rapid, or complex changes can make anyone sweat, whether on the bandstand or in the world at large.

Some musicians love to test themselves against difficult changes. To them, a challenging set of chords is like a maze to navigate without getting lost. Like grandmasters in chess, these players show an enormous capacity to deal with complexity. Floating over the music without making the changes would be like using the pieces on a chessboard to play checkers—it's avoiding the hard work.

The same can be said of making changes in life. Some people truly wrestle with change, whereas others avoid it or simply make cosmetic changes. With the proper attitude, changes in life can move one off a plateau in life and onto a new stage. But many people get caught, say, in a bad job or a bad relationship, and never take the steps to fix it. Others may run from one bad situation to another without making the change they really need to make: the one inside.

Of course, having the ability to make changes is no indication of knowing the Way. A player can know the Way of Zen Guitar through one note just the same as through the most complex harmony. What counts most in this dojo is not the difficulty of one's music, but its spiritual depth.

The true unsui of Zen Guitar become one with the changes. They know that to be fully present in the moment means to be constantly changing like the clouds. If one is fully present in the moment, every change occurs as naturally as the weather. This is the Way of Zen Guitar.

Draw the Frame

I talk to many young painters, because I teach in art schools. I ask them: Why do you think that what you do ends at the edges of this canvas? Think of the frame. What frame are you working in? Not just that bit of wood 'round the edge, but the room you're in, the light you're in, the time and place you're in. How can you redesign it? I would say that to musicians, too. I see them spending a lot of time working on the internal details of what they're doing and far less time working on the ways of positioning it in the world. By "positioning it" I don't only mean thinking of ways of getting it to a record company, but thinking of where it could go, and where it fits in the cultural picture—what else does it relate to?

——Brian Eno

Put two professional photographers in the same room with the same lighting and the same camera, and have each take a picture. The results are likely to be wildly different, depending on how each chooses to compose the shot. By deciding what to include in the shot and what to leave out, and from which perspective to view things, each photographer draws a frame around reality. The skill with which one draws that frame is what separates the artist from the amateur.

Guitar playing requires the same kind of thinking. When you play, you are drawing a frame around a moment and saying to the listener, "Here is how I want you to experience this." How you begin and end a solo is framing. How you structure a song is framing. How you sequence an album is framing. How you present yourself onstage, with what props, is framing.

Framing should heighten the impact of the art, not detract from it. It should give clarity to your vision. There is a reason why good wine tastes better in a wine glass than in a plastic cup, or why hot dogs taste better at a picnic than at a sitdown dinner. The right frame complements the contents.

Understand this and you can make one note seem gigantic if you frame it right. A slight tilt of the frame and something pedestrian reveals itself as something grand.

See every corner of the frame, not just the center. The black belt in this dojo knows that therein lies the measure of artistry.

Zoom In, Zoom Out

*When you're making an album and you have this group of songs,
[they're like] what a newspaper photo looks like if you magnify
it—all you see are dots. . . . Everything seems to be unbelievably
important in its own little tiny thing. [Now that] the album is
done . . . I've been pulling back and zooming out and starting to
see the picture.*

——Tom Hamilton, Aerosmith

The meaning of things differs when seen from close up or
far away. Those who train to the black-belt level here see
as though with a zoom lens, able to move from telescopic detail
to wide-angle perspective in an instant.

One's lens must have the ability to see the smallest ant on the
tree, the tree within the forest, the forest on the mountain, the
mountain range on the continent, the continent on the globe,
and the globe within the universe.

When little problems arise in your playing, widen your lens
angle. If you miss a note, break a string, or can't find your tone,
do not fixate on the problem; it's only one solo, one song, one
gig in the great scheme of your path. Measured against the Way,
all problems seem small. Conversely, when you have trouble focusing, when too many things are on your mind, zoom in close.
Perhaps you're nervous because your parents are in the audience
for the first time, or the deadline for finishing your album is fast

approaching. Put it out of your mind by finding the Way in the smallest detail—playing one note right now.

Develop your sense of perspective. When everything around you looks like weeds, remember: From the heavens, all is a garden.

Then get to weeding.

Trust the Tale

I don't like saying, "You're a punk and you're not." There was a record out over here called "Ça Plane pour Moi" by Plastic Bertrand, right? And I guarantee you if I had it to play for you right now, you'd go, "Right, that is rockin'!" Now, if you were to say to any sort of purist punk, "This is a good punk record," they'd get completely enraged. But Plastic Bertrand, whoever he was, compressed into that three minutes a bloody good record that will get any comatose person toe-tapping, you know what I mean? By purist rules, it's not allowed to even mention Plastic Bertrand. Yet, this record was probably a lot better than a lot of so-called punk records.

——Joe Strummer, The Clash

J once attended a lecture in which a teacher spoke at length about the cultural meaning of a certain popular song. I remember having read an interview with the song's composer, and the teacher's interpretation of it directly contradicted what the composer had said the song was about. I noted this to the teacher.

The teacher said, "Trust the tale, not the teller."

What he meant was, the best art carries a truth all its own. It speaks to us without any need for explanation from artist or critics. If a piece of art has to be understood through the brain first, it has that much further to go to reach the heart.

In an age when musicians are packaged together with their

music, separating tale from teller becomes increasingly difficult. A lot of music today we like because the musicians look good and wear the latest styles, or because we liked the musician's past work. Conversely, a lot of music we ignore because the artists project an image we dislike, their style of music isn't considered hip, or their personal behavior offends our sensibilities. Some famous artists have tried to test this point by submitting works anonymously or under a pseudonym, hoping to have their art stand on its own merits. But audiences seem to feel more comfortable when they have cues to guide their thinking.

As a black belt, be wary of liking or disregarding someone's song simply because of who they are. Don't allow prejudgments to close your mind. Keep your ears open and listen. Even liars can speak the truth, even friends can lead us astray.

Hear the song, not the singer.

Attend to Detail

At the end of a show, he'll leave the stage, and the sirens will be going, and the limousines waiting, and Charlie will walk back to his drumkit and change the position of his drumsticks by two millimeters. Then he'll look at it. Then if it looks good, he'll leave. . . . The drums are about to be stripped down and put in the back of a truck, and he cannot *leave if he's got it in his mind that he's left his sticks in a displeasing way.*
—Keith Richards, on Rolling Stones drummer Charlie Watts

Even in the most trivial matters, there is a right way and a wrong way to do things—a right way to walk on stage, a right way to play one note, a right way to accent one beat. This does not mean what's right for you is right for everyone else. It simply means you should pay attention to every detail and take care to do even the smallest things correctly. Be *mindful* of what you are doing.

How often do we hear ourselves saying, "Where did I put my keys?" or "Have you seen my wallet?" When we don't know the answer, it's because our mind was not in our action. We weren't paying attention to what we were doing.

A zen story tells of a monk named Tenno who had just completed his apprenticeship to become a zen teacher. One rainy day, he went to visit the master Nan-in. As is customary in Japan, Tenno removed his shoes at the vestibule of the master's home.

Nan-in welcomed him and they sat down. After an exchange of greetings, the master asked, "I was wondering, did you leave your umbrella on the left or the right of your shoes?"

The monk could not answer. Of that one detail, he had failed to be mindful—a cardinal sin in zen. Realizing he still lacked zen awareness, he put off teaching and resumed his apprenticeship.

As the saying goes, take care of the little things and the big things take care of themselves. When you set something down, be mindful of where you're setting it. Put things back in their place when you're done with them. If you lay your guitar down the wrong way, pick it up and arrange it the right way. Every action counts.

If you think about it, you can find the Way of Zen Guitar in one detail. The truth in one note is no different from the truth in a symphony.

Thought: Process

How you play a note is just as important as what that note is.
———Henry Kaiser

Many people today are obsessed with the bottom line. We see students who focus on getting the right report-card grades rather than learning; business executives who sacrifice research and development monies for better quarterly profits; musicians who compromise their music in order to land a recording contract.

In this dojo, *there is no bottom line.* How we do something here matters more than the end result. The black-belt guitarist knows to focus on the process, not the product.

Most things in life lie beyond our control—we can't simply snap our fingers and produce the desired result. All we can do is perform our duties the best way we know how. If we do things the right way and our spirit is correct, the results won't matter. We can hold our heads high regardless of the outcome.

In Ernest Hemingway's *The Old Man and the Sea,* the fisherman Santiago goes eighty-four days without catching a fish. Yet throughout the dry spell he stays focused on the process—the proper way to catch a fish. He fishes the right spots. He keeps his lines precisely at the right depth. In this way, he knows the drought is no fault of his own. "I would rather be exact," the old man says. "Then when the luck comes you are ready." This is the way a black belt approaches Zen Guitar.

The process of Zen Guitar is simple: Wear the white belt, pick up your guitar, tune, and play. Focus on putting your spirit into each note and you do not have to worry about landing a record deal or how many albums you sell. If the fish bite, they bite.

Keep refining your process. The Way of Zen Guitar is in the making.

Black Belt Hand

Carriage
Sound Painting
Tone
Intuition
Energy
Yin-Yang
Two Hands as One
Balance

Carriage

You can tell whether [a person] plays or not by the way he carries the instrument, whether it means something to him or not. Then the way they talk and act. If they act too hip, you know they can't play shit.

——Miles Davis

Every move we make in life says something about us, whether we're aware of it or not. Strangers can watch us from a park bench and know something about our character just from the clothes we wear or the way we walk or the way we wear our hair.

The samurai say, "A man who has achieved mastery of an art reveals it in his every action." This is like the jazz musician who says he can tell just from watching the way other musicians set up for a gig whether anything will be "happening" that night.

Those who have achieved the black-belt level in Zen Guitar show it in their very carriage, unself-consciously, before they play a single note.

Sound Painting

Every guitarist has a special quality of sound. The best ones will use a good ear, much sensitivity, and a thorough knowledge of music to prepare the nuances and colors of sound.
———Andrés Segovia

Though we do not see it, sound has color. The black-belt player in this dojo thinks of sound as paint, using the guitar as a paintbrush.

When we speak of musical scales, the very word *chromatic* means of or relating to color. What gives a sound color is its tone and relationship to the notes around it. A painter knows, for example, that a blue placed next to a red looks very different from the same blue placed next to a green. So it is with musical notes. The same note can sound bright or dark when played against different notes. Study the way sonic colors work together to produce various feelings.

When applying color to canvas, some artists throw cans of paint against the wall. Others display a touch as delicate as an eye surgeon. So long as the action is filled with emotional content, either method can work.

See the music like a painter and let the air be your canvas. Then, when you go to the museum, hear the songs that sing on every wall. When all five senses converge to one, you will know the Way of Zen Guitar.

Tone

*I've practiced on my tone for almost . . . 50 years, and if I can't
hear my tone, I can't play. If I can't play, then I won't get paid. If I
don't get paid, then I'll lose the house, you know? It's like a chain
reaction. If I lose my tone, I can't fuck, can't make love, can't do
nothin'. I'll just walk into the ocean and die, if I lose my tone.*

——Miles Davis

A black-belt guitar player is a player who knows tone. On a
sonic level, tone is to sound as hue is to color. A painter
knows there are infinite shades of blue, from the palest baby blue
to the deepest navy. Each shade in the spectrum has its own feeling. Guitar tones are like this. Different tones—clean, distorted,
round, warm—can produce vastly different feelings.

Finding the proper tone can be tricky at times, even for ex-
perienced players. Tone can vary according to the acoustics of
the room, the amplification system, the wood of the guitar, the
gauge of the guitar strings, the material of the pick. Players who
can't find their tone are guaranteed to struggle, like singers with
laryngitis.

On an emotional level, tone also means inflection, as in the
tone of one's voice. Here is where a player must think like an
actor. Where to place the emphasis in a series of notes, the kind
of feeling one puts into the notes—these considerations establish the emotional tone of one's playing. An actor given the

line, "I love you," can render it ten thousand ways, with each reading meaning a different thing. Guitar playing is no different.

Establish the proper tone in everything you do. There is a feeling for every occasion.

Intuition

When I've played from my mind I get in trouble.
>—Stevie Ray Vaughn

In the heat of the moment, there are three things that guide the black-belt player's actions: intellect, instinct, and intuition. Of the three, intuition will best keep you on the path of Zen Guitar.

Intellect calculates and reasons. It bases action on the logic of the conscious mind. But the Way cannot be reduced to reason. One must learn to act in the realm of the illogical.

Instinct reacts without inclusion of the mind. It bases action on innate tendencies. As such, instinct offers the most natural response to any situation, but it can be fooled by the surface of things. That's what leads mice into traps.

Intuition is akin to instinct, but transcends both rational thought and innate tendencies. It bases action not on logic or impulse, but the insight of the unconcious mind. It is a sixth sense that allows us to grasp the truth in things unapparent to the other five senses, and even in the illogical.

If a player gets hit with an unexpected chord change in the heat of the moment, intellect would have us puzzle it out. By the time the mind makes its calculations and gives the body direction, the moment would be lost. One would hear the sound of hesitation.

Instinct usually leads us to the right notes, but can sometimes act too hastily, ignoring experience. The Way of Zen Guitar is to do nothing in haste.

Responding with intuition would mean sensing the unexpected *before it even happens*, and playing the right notes.

When a quarterback gets blitzed in football, if he thinks too much his hesitation will get him sacked. If he acts on instinct and throws too hurriedly, he may get intercepted. With enough experience, though, his intuition warns him that the blitz is coming, and he exploits the situation in the moment.

To develop the intuition of a young samurai named Matajuro, the master swordsman Banzo would creep up and whack him with a wooden sword while he was doing his chores. Day after day Banzo would surprise the apprentice at different moments, until finally, the young man came to sense the master's oncoming attacks before they happened.

Those who train long enough in this dojo learn to trust their intuition above all, knowing the truth of a situation sometimes exists below the surface of things. Develop your intuition in the same way you would your other five senses. Nurture the ability to perceive what cannot be seen or heard, and you will know the feeling of black-belt Zen Guitar.

Energy

You can build a wall to stop people, but eventually, the music, it'll cross that wall. That's the beautiful thing about music—there's no defense against it. I mean, look at Joshua and fuckin' Jericho—made mincemeat of that joint. A few trumpets, you know?

——Keith Richards

When master painters put brush to canvas, a certain energy flows out of their fingertips, through the brush, and into the paint. This energy is apparent to the naked eye—it resides in the very texture of the brushstrokes on the canvas.

Black-belt guitar players know this energy well. It flows through their fingers when fretting and striking a guitar string, and can be heard in the emotional resonance of each note.

In the zen arts, this energy has a name: *ki.*

Ki

Those who call it such know ki as the life force of the universe. It is the thing that makes grass grow, fish swim, birds chirp, babies crawl. Literally in Japanese, ki means "spirit" or "energy." So central is the concept of this energy to the Japanese that it forms the basis of dozens of everyday words, from weather (*tenki*, "heaven energy") to air (*kuki*, "sky energy") to health (*genki*, "source energy").

In the philosophy of ki, the energy that flows through us is something we can direct in very real ways. Japanese gardeners prune a tree with an eye toward enhancing its ki. Chinese acupuncturists place their needles to reroute and stimulate ki through our bodies to relieve pain. Martial artists project their ki with every punch and kick.

Musicians can project their ki outward through sound. When you pick up the guitar, imagine your music flowing through the instrument like water through a hose. Spray the water to the sky. Picture it streaming to the moon and beyond, and your sound will carry.

Those people familiar with ki know it can be developed, like an underused muscle. Concentrate on breathing as slowly as possible over a defined period of time, and you will feel the surge of ki within you.

If you find the idea of ki too mystical, I simply say, "Go with the flow." Live by that phrase in the deepest sense, and you will feel the workings of ki in your life whether you call it by that name or not.

From ki, through ki, with ki. This is the Way of Zen Guitar.

Yin-Yang

When I asked him after the gig, "Miles, what am I supposed to be doing up there?" he said, "When they play fast, you play slow. When they play slow, you play fast."
——Buster Williams, after his first night with Miles Davis

Many Western artists like to speak of their mind as having two halves—a right brain and a left brain. One side controls logic, the other side creativity. In this dojo, we do not speak of right brain–left brain so much as the feeling of *yin* and *yang*.

A cosmological concept that originated in ancient China, yin and yang represent the duality inherent in nature—female and male, night and day, death and birth, matter and void. For every yin there is a yang. The two do not exist independently, but as parts of a whole.

The graphic symbol for yin and yang—interlocking white and black tadpole shapes in a circle—captures the essence of the idea. The white half contains a small circle of black; the black half contains a small circle of white. That is to say, there are circles within circles within circles, and within everything yin there is a bit of yang, within everything yang there is a bit of yin. You can find the Way through this idea alone.

陰
陽

Yin-yang

The interplay of yin and yang exists in all the dynamics of music—call and response, tension and release, sound and silence. Yang calls, yin responds. Yang builds tension, yin releases it. Yang is the note; yin is the space between notes. This dynamic is what gives the music its vitality.

Feel yin-yang in every aspect of your life, down to the smallest detail, and your music will only deepen. Whether inside this dojo or out, yin-yang is always there. It is not two. It is one.

Two Hands as One

My right hand is flashier than my left hand. My left hand tends to want to play straight-up melodies. My right hand wants to play too many notes. Somewhere in between it all comes together.
———Bill Kirchen,
Commander Cody and His Lost Planet Airmen

Most of us grow up right-handed or left-handed. We bring this attitude to the guitar as beginners—that is, we tend to focus on what one hand is doing to the exclusion of the other.

Even though one hand is fretting the strings and the other is striking them, you must not think of each hand individually. They are part of the same whole. Recognize the oneness in the duality of right and left. It will help you understand yin and yang.

Harmonizing body and mind requires each hand to know what the other is doing at all times. This is true in every endeavor.

Balance

I tried to play in front of the beat in a way that didn't rush it, or behind the beat in a way that didn't drag it.

——Rick Danko, The Band

Those who follow the path of Zen Guitar must develop a delicate sense of balance—a sensitivity to nuance and small degrees that deepens each step of the path. One develops this sense of balance by establishing a strong center. The samurai call it *chudan*—literally, middle ground.

To occupy chudan is to know the feeling of total balance—physical, mental, and spiritual. From chudan, our spirit is free to move forward, backward, left, right, up, or down. Whichever way we move from chudan, that in itself becomes chudan. It is an instant adjustment.

Chudan

Basketball players, for example, keep their dribble options open so they can go right or left. This is chudan. Once they commit to a direction, the defense adjusts. The skilled dribbler then adjusts to the adjustment, creating a new opportunity to go right or left—back to chudan. This happens in an instant. Never losing the center means never losing balance.

Maintaining proper balance is critical in all levels of performance. Tone should not be too dull or too shrill; volume should not be too loud or too faint; rhythm should not lag too far or rush too fast; tension should not build overlong and release should not come too soon.

One's statement should exhibit balance as well. It should have integrity and honesty without being overearnest, stay true to its own vision without being self-indulgent, show the Way but not be preachy. There's a fine line between celebrating the song and celebrating the self.

The only way to find chudan is through practice and experience. Sometimes that means crossing a line before we know where it is, but those are the risks of exploration. Many are the musicians who have crossed the line from, say, drug use to abuse. Some make it back with vital self-knowledge and a healthy respect for the line. Some never return.

Those with a feeling for chudan know that the difference between balance and disproportion can be a hair's breadth. Bending a note just *slightly* too far, holding a note just *slightly* too long, hitting a note just *slightly* too soon—these hairs diminish the impact of one's actions like the fraction of an inch on a baseball bat that separates a pop-up from a home run. Know the measure of a hair's breadth; therein lies the Way.

Chudan does not mean, however, that one occupies the exact middle of a place. It does not, for example, require a musician to play only on the beat. From chudan, we can make the decision to ride the beat or play behind the beat. But we still do so the chudan way—not *too* far behind the beat when playing behind, not *too* ahead of the beat when riding it. Maintain your center, even in disproportion.

When driving up to a yellow light, sometimes we speed up, sometimes we slow down. It depends on our center at that moment. So long as we do everything with a feeling of chudan, we stay on the path of Zen Guitar.

Black Belt Heart

True Self
Conviction
Jamming
Recording
First Take
Virtuosity
Mastery

True Self

Playing the guitar is like telling the truth—you never have to worry about repeating the same [lie] if you told the truth. You don't have to pretend, or cover up. If someone asks you again, you don't have to think about it or worry about it . . . because there it is. It's you.
——B. B. King

It has been said that in modern life we will each have our fifteen minutes of fame. If that is so, when the spotlight swings your way, do not shy from it. Step into it and show what you're made of.

Prepare yourself, because in this world of instant celebrity, privacy is a thin veneer. One chance occurrence—tragedy or good fortune—can propel you in front of the nation. You must be ready for this at any moment.

The way to prepare yourself is to live life the same regardless of who's watching—with integrity. Be who you are and do what you do and you will have no need to put on airs for people. Your actions will be appropriate to the occasion because they'll be true.

Whether living in the spotlight or alone in the woods, show true humility and grace and you will know what it means to play Zen Guitar. You will not hesitate to answer when the philosopher asks, "If a tree falls in a forest and no one is around to hear it, does it still make a sound?"

"Yes," you'll say. "It makes the sound of one hand clapping."

Conviction

I don't care who likes it or buys it. Because if you use that criterion, Mozart would have never written Don Giovanni, *Charlie Parker would never have played anything but swing music. There comes a point at which you have to stand up and say, this is what I have to do.*

——Branford Marsalis

Your playing must have conviction. It should show the measure of your belief in what you know to be true, to the point where you would stake your life on it.

Many skilled guitarists play music they don't care for. They ply their trade for money, turning in polished performances, all in a day's work. Sometimes they like the music they're asked to play; sometimes they're indifferent; sometimes they hate it.

Other skilled players reach a certain level of success and become complacent. Their playing lacks the fire of their youth, the hunger of their earlier struggles.

In Zen Guitar, your inner fire must always show through. Play from the inside out; your sound should stem from the conviction of the soul. This is what makes vital music.

A wise man once said that a person who has nothing to die for hasn't a life worth living. On the path of Zen Guitar, you must take this to heart. In the years leading up to the fall of communism in Czechoslovakia, rock groups played their music knowing it meant imprisonment. Their defiance spawned the dissident movement that eventually brought down the government. When played with total conviction, the guitar has that kind of power.

We all must find that thing we stand for in this life, and, if necessary, go to our death defending. It may be a person or a place, a principle or an ideal. When you find it, play your music with the spirit of the bagpiper leading Scottish troops into battle—eyes fixed straight ahead, propelled forward by song. That is playing the truth in the face of all opposition.

Do not look to be a martyr, though. As J. D. Salinger noted in *The Catcher in the Rye,* "The mark of the immature man is that he wants to die nobly for a cause, while the mark of the mature man is that he wants to live humbly for one." Be willing to die for your music, but more important: *live* for it.

Jamming

The most important thing I look for in a musician is whether he knows how to listen.

—Duke Ellington

Some players perform strictly unaccompanied. Others perform in groups, but play only prewritten parts. To achieve a black belt in Zen Guitar, one must know the spirit of jamming—how to improvise with other players in the moment.

To truly jam, you must subjugate your ego for the good of the group and seek a harmony that lifts everyone higher. One player acting selfishly can ruin a jam. In basketball, for example, if one player on a team hogs the ball and takes all the shots, the other players become selfish and start hogging the ball as well. But if a player thinks first of passing the ball and setting others up to score, others begin to think the same. Just as selfish attitudes are contagious, so are generous ones. If you play generously, anyone who's listening will feel it.

It is said that music is the only language where many people can talk at once and be understood. But there are still rules for conversing. Effective jamming means knowing how to listen, when to lead, and when to follow. There is no rule more basic to functioning in a group setting.

Listening

If you've ever been to a country where you don't speak the language, you know how difficult it is to communicate. You must look for people who are generous and willing to try and understand you. They must fully concentrate on your efforts at communication; you must fully concentrate on theirs. What you're looking for is a bridge that will carry you across the divide. When you find it, what develops is a kind of third language—not your tongue and not the other's, but a hybrid of the two. The shared spirit of trying to communicate is what carries you along to that common ground where you can make yourselves understood.

Musicians jam in the same way. No matter what their different styles, backgrounds, or preferences, players who know how to jam can make themselves understood. They're always looking for the bridge—musically and figuratively.

Leading

A jam will not go anywhere unless someone takes the lead. It need not be the same person throughout; in fact, different people can take the lead at different points within the same number. But if no one steps forward and says, "This is where we should go," the music will meander, wasting everyone's time.

Determining who should lead at any given point can be difficult. Sometimes the leader is preestablished—the person who calls the jam, for example, or the person whose home it's in. Other times the leader is the person with the most experience, or the most respected level of ability. Or the leader can be someone who simply has the strongest vision of where the jam should go.

Conflict can arise when two or more people vie for leadership at the same time. Sometimes this can produce creative tension that lifts the group higher. More often, these ego battles destroy group cohesion. The same can be said of situations where the leader does not command respect. The music simply will not get to the highest place it can go.

When leading, don't fixate on what the other players can't do; work with what they can do. Jams fail when one player can't get past the limitations of another. It may mean altering your vision for that moment, but good leaders don't seek to make people fit into an existing model. They adjust and build a new model out of the pieces they have.

Following

Even a leader must know how to follow. Sometimes, supporting players can suggest new directions worth following at a moment's notice. Other times, a jam calls for round-robin leadership, where players alternate between leading and following. Then there are times when you're sitting in on someone else's gig and it just isn't your jam to lead.

When following, do so in the spirit of fitting in, in whatever way lifts the group highest. Sometimes this means playing something less than the full extent of your ability. But if that's what lifts the music up, do it. The best musician is not the one with the best chops, but the one who best knows how to contribute to the whole.

Fitting in with others does not mean relinquishing your individuality. In fact, if the spirit of the jam is right, your uniqueness is your asset. Be like the hot sauce in a jambalaya—an indispensable spice that adds to the character of the whole.

Listen, lead, and follow. Carry this spirit to all your relationships and make your song the biggest jam in the world. That is the Way of Zen Guitar.

Recording

I think musicians, as they grow older, usually become interested in doing something more lasting. . . . You've just got to settle down and make everything count and make sure that it's worthy of being heard again, not just a throwaway.

——Eric Clapton

A record is simply that: a document of a moment in time. As such, it can be quickly discarded, or last through the ages.

What a record contains is your spirit—your soul, your energy, your emotion, your thoughts, your passion, your sorrow, your rhythm, your sensibility, your strength, your weakness—the very breath of your life. Like a genie, your spirit in that moment is bottled forever, to be let loose again and again by anyone who so desires.

Some recordings contain a spirit so deep and profound they reward endless listening. These recordings actually change people's lives—people the artist never sees or knows, years after the artist's death. Such an experience can lead future generations to find the Way.

Carry the spirit of recording to anything that documents your life: diaries, paintings, photographs, writings, the house you built, the essays you wrote for high school English class. These records are a message from the past to the future. What do you want them to say about yourself? Will they inspire those yet unborn?

Consider this deeply before you commit yourself to record. Then, when the red recording light goes on, be in it with your whole self.

First Take

They just said, "Roll the tape." No rehearsal or nothing. . . .
Muddy [Waters] didn't come in and say, "I wanna rehearse." He
used to look at me and say, "Let's just play the blues. That's all
you need to do."

——Buddy Guy

When musicians record, they often perform several versions of the same song and choose the best one. Movie directors do the same thing, shooting the same scene several times until they get one exactly the way they want.

Why is it that, even when all the notes are the same in each take, or the same lines are read by the same actors, one version stands out above the others? For the same reason a golfer can hit a dozen balls and one shot will land closer to the hole. Human beings are not machines. Timing, mechanics, and emotional content differ ever so slightly with each take. Every rendition, every pass through, is a distinct moment in time never to be repeated in exactly the same way. This is what's meant by the saying, "You never step into the same river twice."

Feel this in your heart and relate it to whatever you do in life. No matter how many times the song gets played, the black-belt Zen Guitarist knows each version is the first—and only—take.

Every note you play, everything you do: It's all one take.

Virtuosity

Whether you are [playing] in the bar, the church, the strip joint, or the Himalayas, the first duty of music is to complement and enhance life.

—Carlos Santana

When people speak of virtuosity these days, they describe a kind of super ability, a dazzling technical excellence. But what's missing from this definition is the root of the word: *virtue.*

In the Zen Guitar Dojo, the virtuoso players are the ones who rise above technical mastery and exhibit true virtue in every note they play—honesty, integrity, charity, gratitude, compassion. To them, music becomes more than a personal release or ecstasy. It serves to create harmony in the broadest sense of the word. These players are the true guitar heroes.

Like heroes in other cultures, the black-belt Zen Guitarist is a noble warrior. This is why we call the guitar an "axe"—because it has all the power of a weapon in battle. Our work here teaches us to use that power responsibly.

When samurai warriors train to perfect a deadly technique with the sword, they come to understand the fleetingness of life. This is why master samurai speak of wielding a "life-giving sword"—one that respects the preciousness of every breath, knowing how near we always walk to death.

So, too, must the Zen Guitarist carry a life-giving axe. Understand and respect the depth of your instrument's power. The guitar has the capacity to save lives; it has given many a desperate person reason to go on. Use its power wisely.

Wield your axe with beauty and virtue, and carry a noble heart.

Peace through Zen Guitar.

Mastery

You have to persist, and out of the sheer frustration of what you've been doing or you haven't been doing you just come out the other side. Of course, when you come out the other side, you find that there's an even bigger hill to climb than the last one.

——Allan Holdsworth

The first rule of mastery is this: Those who think themselves masters are not masters.

There can be no letup of your study, no matter how far you've come. Even the highest priests of zen say to themselves, *mi zai*: "Not yet." You have not yet learned all you can know. You have not yet given all you can give. You have not yet reached the summit.

Empty your cup and keep going. Same mountain, farther up.

Mi zai

黒 白

Kuro-Shiro: Black-White

barrier

You've got to be able to hold a lot of contradictory ideas in your mind without going nuts. I feel like to do my job right, when I walk out onstage I've got to feel like it's the most important thing in the world. Also I've got to feel like, well, it's only rock and roll. Somehow you've got to believe both of those things.

——Bruce Springsteen

A famous zen saying describes the journey to enlightenment this way:

First step, mountain is mountain.
Second step, mountain is not mountain.
Third step, mountain is mountain.

So it is with music on the path of Zen Guitar.

Before we set foot on the path, music is just music to us—something we enjoy without having to think about. But once we dedicate ourselves to playing, music becomes something more. On this second step, music is not music so much as our passion, our sweat, our soul, our religion. With everything we learn, its beauty only becomes more mysterious.

After a time, those of a certain mind begin to ask, Where is this music coming from? Am I channeling it? From where? What is driving me to play it? How deep does it go? If these are your questions and you sincerely seek enlightenment, the third step holds your answers. This is where you must see through to the very essence of music—what music *is*. Do that and you'll come face-to-face with the source of all sound: the sound of one hand clapping, *sekishu no onjo*. There, the masters tell us, you'll see through to the source of your own existence—the source of all that ever was, is, and will be. Every question in your life, every doubt, and every craving will vanish. You will awaken to your true nature. You will know the Way of Zen Guitar.

This final leap can take a lifetime, or it can happen right now.

All that stands in the way is a barrier—not a physical one, but one of the mind. It is the barrier at the end of thinking, where logic can go no further. Zen masters call it *mu*.

Mu

Mu, in Japanese, means "no thing," or "the absence of a thing." It does not mean "nothing," for in zen, nothing is still something. Rather, zen masters say mu is a timeless void transcending rational comprehension, the point where all senses come together. Out of this mu, they say, flows the stream of time and all that exists.

When zen masters ask, "What is the sound of one hand clapping?" they do so knowing there is no way to answer logically. The question is a *koan*, a riddle designed to force the transcendence of rationality.

As rational beings, we see only the dual nature of reality.

Something either exists or it doesn't. There's a guitar in our hands or there isn't. We hear sound or we hear silence. There is you and there is me, and there is the space between us. Rationally, this is the truth.

Zen masters tell us that mu transcends such duality, revealing not only the oneness of all things, but the void at its source. Mu, they say, is the source of the note *and* the silence, while at the same time being neither. You say this doesn't make sense to you? Of course it doesn't. Mu lies beyond the limits of logical understanding—at the place of no words, no form, and no mind.

Enlightened ones liken this mu to a gateless gate. It is a gate because we must pass through it in order to know the ultimate truth of things. Yet at the same time, it is gateless, because we already *embody* the truth of all things; no passageway to the truth is necessary because we already *hold* the truth. We need only to awaken to the fact of our true nature.

Somehow, we must penetrate this mu. The only way, zen masters say, is to focus on the moment so hard and relentlessly that the mind ceases all wandering and words disappear. In this dojo, that means focusing on each note until we can see it, smell it, touch it, and taste it.

When we enter this world from the womb, all sensation is pure sensation. There are no words in our head. The voice of our mother, the light of the sun, the smell of the rain—all of it is one great sensation, flowing in a continuous stream. We *see* sound, we *hear* feelings, we *taste* light, because it is all the same. The moment we begin distinguishing sight from sound from smell, separating things, naming and categorizing them, we begin the rational process that leads us away from experiencing true oneness.

Zen Guitar is a means by which we return to our original senses. To experience sound again as though newly born—therein lies the ultimate beginner's mind.

This is not to deny the place of rationality. I have said before, we only become human in relation to the space around us, even though to see the relationship of things—us to others, matter to void—is the essence of dual thinking. The fundamental challenge of zen is to realize mu without denying the fact of duality; it is a basic principle of zen that "things are not what they seem, nor are they otherwise."

Having said all that, let me make clear: Zen Guitar is not an exercise in navel-gazing. The Way is not to be found through self-consciousness, but *un*self-consciousness. "If you seek it," the masters say, "you will not find it." All you ever need do on the path is wear the white belt, pick up your guitar, tune, and play. If you play what you're meant to play, giving of yourself, naturally, in the moment, you will know the essence of zen. Mu will not matter.

In this section, I offer some thoughts on Six Dualities, far along the path of Zen Guitar, where the unsui should intuitively perceive the way to make two into one. They are:

1. Entrance and exit
2. Perfection and imperfection

3. I and thou
4. Holding on and letting go
5. Sound and silence
6. Teacher and student

If you travel this stretch of the path, your black belt will fray to the point of whiteness.

Entrance and Exit

Music should go right through you, leave some of itself inside you, and take some of you with it when it leaves.

——Henry Threadgill

When people are in a state of confusion, we say they don't know whether they're coming or going. On the path of Zen Guitar there should be no such confusion.

As a rule, each step should have a feeling of entrance. This is the beginner's mind—the state of *becoming*. In the zen arts, there is a saying that applies: "Enter by form, exit from form." It has meaning on many levels.

In the dojo, we "enter by form" when we diligently learn all the rules of music—theory, scales, harmony, technique, and so on. We "exit from form" when, having internalized the rules, we throw them all out and just play.

Onstage, we enter by form playing a straight piece of music, the way it was written or, as the case may be, recorded. We exit from form when we improvise out of what's written and go into uncharted territory. We can also exit if we bring such intensity to the form that we transcend it.

Even in life, we enter by form—our physical bodies. We exit from form when those bodies expire, or right here, through enlightenment by means of Zen Guitar.

In many people's minds, the idea of entrance and exit implies a kind of closure. We start and finish a song. We play a gig and go home. We record an album and release it. But remember, the path of Zen Guitar goes on forever. In life, as in music, some things just fade out to infinity.

On the deepest level, we must look to transcend the duality of entrance and exit, for to truly live in the moment means entrance and exit are simultaneous. There is no entering of one moment and exiting on to the next. There just *is*.

No entrance, no exit. Only the Way.

Perfection and Imperfection

I'll go for things that I know are going to be wrong, with a vengeance.

—Neil Young

In the Zen Guitar Dojo, we spend countless hours in pursuit of perfection—the perfect tone, the perfect technique, the perfect recording. It is only through this pursuit that we come to know the poetry of imperfection.

Sometimes the note bent slightly below pitch carries more impact than the one dead on, or the squeal of unexpected feedback has just the right character. Poetic imperfection is the crooked twist in the stem of a flower, the asymmetrical line of the handcrafted bowl, the knot in the piece of wood, the mole at the corner of a lip, the moon partially obscured by clouds. Somehow, the presence of these "imperfections" serves to heighten the beauty in nature, not detract from it.

To go beyond the black-belt level in Zen Guitar, you must develop a keen sense to realize when imperfection is perfection. Know when to leave well enough alone.

I and Thou

*Sometimes . . . you would feel this presence together with the au-
dience and the band, which was just such a mindblower. It felt
better than the other gigs. You felt some sort of connection, where
there was a whole wave of five or ten thousand people coming at
you; you felt that you and the audience were actually one.*

——Ringo Starr

As I have said, the Way of Zen Guitar requires that our
music make a connection outside of ourselves. But
what is the point of this connection? It is communion.

Whether communing with the audience, other band mem-
bers, or one's personal god, Zen Guitar seeks the fusion of spir-
its into a larger whole—to transcend the relationship of I and
thou to create one, us and all.

Music is the means to this transcendence. When striking a
fortunate harmony, we see through our separateness as the
spirit of player and listener flows into one great sea. It is the
feeling of the Way surging through—beyond the capacity of
words to describe, yet instantly understood to be the truth. It is
a collective epiphany.

Do not aim for this kind of communion as a goal. Just play
with an open heart and let it come. If your song is pure, it will
be like a runway to the truth. Play it without thought to pur-
suing transcendence, and you will naturally lift off.

Your manner should be as though inviting the listener into

your home. Draw from the spirit of the Japanese tea ceremony, an art in which the act of a host serving tea and a guest gratefully receiving it form a model for all human relations. The host shows the guest every consideration; the guest expresses gratitude for the host's generosity. Tea is the conduit through which they commune together and all of life fuses in the singleness of the moment.

So it should be when playing Zen Guitar for an audience. Play for others as though they were in your living room and offer them your song as you would a bowl of tea: from the generosity of your heart, with no expectation of reciprocity.

This is not so simple as it may seem. First the audience must accept your invitation. Many will reject it. Hurtful as that may be, you cannot impose your music on those who don't want it, even if you think what you're offering is good for them. Some people won't listen.

There will be people who accept your invitation, then disrespect your offering. This can upset the enjoyment of those who truly want to hear. When the heckler boos, when the lout breaks a silence, you must endeavor to make harmony from this disharmony, if only in the smallest way. Jazz musicians like to say you can play any note against any other note as long as you *resolve* it. This is true in human relations as well. The way to bring harmony from disharmony is through total resolution. When differences arise, show your compassion and do not reciprocate disrespect with disrespect. The samurai say if you harbor ill thoughts during peace, you will bring war; if you harbor pure thoughts during war, you will bring peace. Like the spirit

Ichigo ichie

of nonviolent resistance, the pursuit of harmony requires far more strength than hatred. You must have the strength to wage peace.

Treat each audience with each person as something precious. In the tea ceremony, host and guest call this *ichigo ichie*—one time, one meeting. Each gathering is a special occasion. Though we may perform the same song ten thousand times, each is a once-in-a-lifetime occurrence. Player and listener experience the moment together and it passes. You may play for the same group of friends again and again, or there may be one person in the crowd you never see, who has saved for a month, driving all night just to hear you play your song. You cannot give anything less to the moment than your total spirit.

In the spirit of ichigo ichie, all the energy you send out comes back from your guests multiplied for you to send out again. Through this circle, we transcend the separateness of "I" and "thou" to reveal the one. This is the Way of Zen Guitar.

Holding On and Letting Go

*I lose myself at some point during almost every musical perfor-
mance. There's some point of struggle and super self-consciousness,
but I always get lost at some point. While I'm playing, there's a
pattern of struggling through something and then cracking
through it by a weird combination of willpower and letting go.
That's the most enjoyable thing for me: "Uh-oh, he's gone!"*

—David Torn

J was talking with an artist friend once at a gallery opening
for his rock sculptures. I asked whether he would miss
not having his favorite works around once buyers had purchased them.

He scoffed. "I could take these stones and throw them in the
bottom of the ocean," he said.

He meant it. His joy came not from the objects but the work
itself. It was the *act* of creation, not the creation itself, that gave
his life meaning.

The same should be true for those who play Zen Guitar. Like
loving parents who bring a child into the world, we pour heart
and soul into creating something knowing we must let go. To
hold on is to live with fear, ego, and selfishness. Letting go
means to transcend those things and follow the path of growth.

A famous zen parable about letting go tells of a dying master,
Mu-nan, who seeks to bequeath a cherished, handwritten
scripture book to his disciple Shoju.

At first, Shoju refused the gift. "If the book is such an important thing," he said, "you had better keep it." But the master insisted and put it in Shoju's hand.

Shoju accepted it and laid it on the flaming coals of the brazier.

"What are you doing!?" the master shouted.

"What are you saying?" came the reply.

In letting go, we implicitly acknowledge life's impermanence. Nothing material lasts forever—least of all our material being. In the long run, all will be dust.

The paradox is that by letting go, we hold on to the very thing that is permanent: not the song, but the source of the song. Therein lies the Way.

The player who truly lets go is like a mirror reflecting the beautiful light of the moon—holding nothing, illuminating everything.

Sound and Silence

It doesn't matter if you're the greatest guitar player in the world, if you're not enlightened, forget it.

——George Harrison

For centuries, wandering monks in Japan have played the *shakuhachi,* a traditional bamboo flute, for the purposes of meditation. The sound has been likened to that of deer calling one another.

The measure of artistry with the shakuhachi is *ichion jobutsu*—the quality of enlightenment in one note. To the shakuhachi player, every note and every space between the notes has equal importance to every other, because there is no sound without silence and no silence without sound. Nothing—not a single breath through the flute—can go to waste. In the mind of a shakuhachi master, each moment in this world has its distinct existence and then is gone forever; each sound and each silence is an opportunity for enlightenment.

一音成仏

Ichion jobutsu

A story goes that, hundreds of years ago, the Japanese emperor asked a monk named Kakua to teach what he had learned on a zen retreat to China. The monk bowed, stood silently, played one note on his shakuhachi and departed.

In that one note, he showed his enlightenment.

Apply the spirit of ichion jobutsu to everything you play. If you penetrate deeply enough, you will come to realize the place of no sound and no silence, and your guitar will speak the truth. Ichion jobutsu is what you're after.

Teacher and Student

You get older . . . you start having hopes for other people rather than yourself.

——Bob Dylan

It is said that in any given situation, someone is doing the teaching and someone is doing the learning. This thinking is central to the Way of Zen Guitar.

We are all students and teachers in everything we do, and we are both at the same time. When a child learns from the parent, the parent learns from the child. Each imparts different lessons. We teach the child about the ways of the world while the child teaches us the innocence and wonder of learning. There is nothing more fundamental to life.

In this dojo, you have an obligation to fulfill each role. As an unsui, you must maximize your potential. Seek out knowledge and thirst for it wherever you can find it, letting all things be your teacher. You must go so far as to, in the words of the samurai, "climb on the shoulders of the teacher."

The farther you advance on your path, the more you become a *sensei*—one who has gone before. As a sensei, you must share what you've learned on your journey with those coming up behind you, and realize that everything you do, even unconsciously, teaches by example. This is your responsibility to the Way of Zen Guitar, and to the next generation.

If you take this responsibility seriously, your teaching will inform your learning, just as your learning will inform your teaching. Your unsui mind will know the confusion of learning something new; then, as a sensei, you can empathize with your student. Your sensei mind will know the most effective way to transfer knowledge; then, as an unsui, you can look for these qualities when seeking your teacher.

Of all the things you do in this dojo, your actions as sensei may be most important. You must show young people a true example of Zen Guitar. You cannot divorce what you do here from the surrounding world.

All around young people today is the violence of modern life—abandonment, abuse, intimidation. Many young people live in broken families. Some come from places where their schools don't work. They might have spiritless teachers or apathetic classmates. So many negative forces work on the psyche of youth today that thousands lack the self-esteem to even see their own strength in the mirror.

Music can change these lives—*any* lives—for the better. I have seen young people for whom music is the reason to go on living. It eases the pain of life and provides a source of joy.

I established this dojo because I believe anything that encourages people to pick up the guitar is a good thing. Give them six strings and a slab of wood and you've given them a sense of identity and a voice in the world. *Everyone* has a song to sing—that's a bedrock principle of Zen Guitar.

But too much of the music being made today promotes dubious values—instant gratification and ego glorification. Popular artists espouse messages of disaffection and alienation, glorifying guns, misogyny, and suicide, turning ignorance into a badge of honor.

Some people say this rebelliousness is an inherent part of youth culture, others say it reflects the truth of modern life. But those who travel the path of Zen Guitar must offer an alternative—true alternative music. Your song must say we need not always celebrate our animal impulses; we can rise above them. Your actions as sensei must guide students to see Zen Guitar as a means of empowerment.

"When the student is ready," zen masters say, "the teacher will appear." See the dual meaning here. This dojo appeared in your life when you were ready for its teaching. Now you must be ready for the teacher to appear in you.

Please, take responsibility and encourage young people not to follow in your path or someone else's, but to forge their own. Let them know through song and deed that the possibility of transcendence—the experience of eternity—exists here and now. Once they make that discovery, all of life starts to produce a feeling of aliveness, down to a single note on a single string.

Show them your belt is as white as theirs. ○

Shiro: White

the way of zen guitar

Return to the beginning.
Enter by form.
Clean your dojo.
As you have every day, tie on the white belt and empty your cup.
Pick up your guitar, tune, then play.

Feel the rhythm in nature and move to it.
That which you make, make as well as you can.
Sound and resound.
Learn why you're here.
Seek the truth as an unsui, floating and flowing.
Delay gratification; lengthen the attention span.
Take joy in the struggle.
Hear like a mother alert to the cry of her child.
Speak directly from your heart to the heart of your listener,
*   as if passing the flame of a candle.*

Understand ch'iyun, and feel it.
Play what you hear, and hear what you play.
Serve your soul.
Study yourself.
Master your deeds.
Know the feeling of shouting at the waves crashing ashore.
Spur your spirit like a running horse.
Put one foot in front of the other. Repeat.

Learn how to do something.
Do something, then learn what you did.
Clap your hands like a child. Sing a naive melody.
Trust your ears.
Harden the stomach of your sound.
Develop one good habit.
Check your path. Check it again.
Focus on what you're doing to the point it becomes unconscious.
Synchronize with many rhythms.

Breathe in.

Breathe out.

Repeat slowly, then go slower.
Continue for fifteen minutes. Tomorrow, go sixteen.

Understand hyoshi, and feel it.
Put your accidents to creative use.

Grow like a tree—toward the light.
Pay attention to the task at hand.
Know why you practice.
Do what has to be done, when it has to be done.
Do a little more, and do not stop for your whole lifetime.
Tighten your mind.

Move through the stages and plateaus.
Step lively at a natural pace.
Write a phrase on the blackboard ten thousand times and
  believe it.
In one stroke, draw the largest perfect circle you can.
Float like a ball on a river.
If you go against the current, swim like a carp.
Compete with yourself. The only opponent is within.
Acquire the technique you need and no more.
Run like a marathoner, right through the finish line.
Know when to speed up and when to slow down.
Be quick, not hasty.

See both hands as one.
Avoid overthinking. Rely on the memory and intelligence of
  your muscles.
Stick with what works best, but add new wrinkles.
Know how to play big at low volume, and quiet at high
  volume.
Turn a wince into a smile. When things fall apart, make art.
Push hard against your limits and learn them well.

Show excellent taste.
Fall like a cat. Say, "I'm lucky to be alive."
Draw one continuous line. Do not cross over it and do not stop.
Build up instead of tearing down.
Know when building up sometimes means tearing down.

Band together. Lean into the curves with others like lugers.
Surround yourself with people of character.
Cherish good chemistry.
Add two and two to make one.
Do not chase two rabbits at once.
Work not to become the best player, but the best person.
Get to the bottom of your song. From that, know ten thousand
things.

When you sit, sit like a mountain—immovable.
When you rise, rise like the sun—unstoppable.
Extend your ki.
Play with the purity of a bird calling in the wild.
Put your ego in its place. Never underestimate its power to lead
you astray.
Measure a compliment the same as you measure a critique.
Do not think you've arrived.
Carry yourself naturally. If you know it, you will show it.
Make a statement with sonority.
Maximize the kokoro ire.
Narrow your focus and expand your mind.
Feel the circles within and without, to infinity.

Delete needless notes.
Repeat: Delete needless notes.

Prepare to meet your death. When the moment comes, there is no
*   time for thinking.*
Trust your intuition. Perceive that which you cannot see or hear.
Announce your presence at the front door.
At the back door, enter quietly.

Know the feeling of power held in reserve.
Set the right tone.
Paint with sound. Show your touch.
Spray your music outward like water through a hose.
Understand yin-yang, and feel it.
Know the measure of a hair's breadth when you play.
Go up to the line and do not be afraid.

Take care to do the small and trivial things.
Get to the bridge and cross it.
Know how to listen, lead, and follow. Jam with as many people
*   as possible.*
Fit in uniquely.
Understand chudan, and feel it.
Recognize the truth when you hear it.

Beware of false teachers.
Make the first take the best. You only get one.
Strip away illusion. Retain the mystery.

Draw the frame with a mind to every corner.
See the ant within the universe, and the universe within the ant.
Invite a listener to the biggest living room in the world—yours.
Weed your garden.

Keep going. When you go beyond, keep going. Mi zai, mi zai.

Offer your song freely.
Make the deep changes.
Live as a ningen.
Accept responsibility.
Play from the inside out, with a noble heart.

Ride the analog waves like a surfer.
Arrange the digital bits like a collagist.
Do not aim for transcendence through your song. Just play and
let it come.
Open your mind to imperfection.
Give without regard to getting. Receive with sincere gratitude.
Perform in the spirit of ichigo ichie.
Show your strength through compassion.
Do not proselytize your way of life. Seek not to save those who
don't want to be saved.

See the glass as half full. Understand that as
you try to fill it, the glass will get bigger.
Endeavor to make harmony from disharmony.
Measure yourself through ichion jobutsu.

Study those before you; encourage those behind you.
Combine beauty with virtue.
Own nothing, illuminate everything.
Exit from form.
Awaken.

Fix these words in your heart and you will know the silence within and without every note you play.

It is the sound of one hand clapping.

ZEN GUITAR

Glossary

Ch'iyun: Sympathetic vibration of the vital spirit; "spirit source" or "energy origin."

Chudan: Center of balance; literally, "middle ground."

Dojo: A training hall, practice ground, or school devoted to refinement of the spirit; "place of the Way."

Hyoshi: Natural rhythm; literally, "child's clap."

Ichion jobutsu *(ee-chee-own jyo-boot-soo)***:** The quality of enlightenment in one note; "one sound, Buddha become."

Ichigo ichie *(ee-chee-go ee-chee-eh)***:** Literally, "One time, one meeting," meaning an opportunity for experience that will never come again.

Katsu: A shout that emanates from the soul.

Ki: Spirit/energy of the cosmos.

Kiki: Crisis; literally, "danger occasion/opportunity."

Koan: A zen riddle or problem that cannot be solved by logic.

Kokoro ire _(ee-rhe)_: Inclusion of the heart's spirit.

Mi zai: Not yet; translates directly as "dwelling immature."

Mu: Empty, void, no-thing; zen's gateway to enlightenment.

Ningen: Human being; literally, "person space/interval."

Sekishu no onjo _(seh-ki-shoo no own-jyo)_: A zen koan meaning, The sound of one hand clapping. Direct translation is, "One hand of a pair, sound's voice."

Sensei: Teacher; literally, "preceding in growth" or "previous in life."

Shugyo _(shoo-gyo)_: Training; "mastering deeds."

Suki: Interval, gap.

Unsui _(oon-soo-ee)_: Truth seeker or training monk; literally, "cloud and water," a reference to the flowing, floating spirit required in training.

Select Bibliography

Books

Addiss, Stephen. *The Art of Zen*. New York: Harry N. Abrams, 1989.

Addiss, Stephen, and G. Cameron Hurst III. *Samurai Painters*. Tokyo: Kodansha International, 1983.

Campbell, Joseph with Michael Toms. *An Open Life*. San Francisco: Larson Publications, 1988.

Campbell, Joseph with Bill Moyers. *The Power of Myth*. New York: Doubleday, 1988.

Deshimaru, Taisen. *Questions to a Zen Master*. New York: Arkana, 1981.

Funakoshi, Gichin. *Karate-Do: My Way of Life*. Tokyo: Kodansha International, 1975.

Grigg, Ray. *The New Lao Tzu*. Rutland, Vermont: Charles E. Tuttle, 1995.

Herrigel, Eugen. *Zen in the Art of Archery*. New York: Vintage Books, 1953.

Herrigel, Gustie L. *Zen in the Art of Flower Arrangement*. London: Arkana, 1958.

Hoffmann, Yoel. *The Sound of the One Hand*. New York: Basic Books, 1973.

Hyams, Joe. *Zen in the Martial Arts*. New York: Bantam Books, 1979.

Kaufman, Hanshi Steve. *The Martial Artist's Book of Five Rings*. Boston: Charles E. Tuttle, 1994.

Lao Tzu. *The Way of Life*. Trans. R. B. Blakney. New York: Mentor, 1955.

Liang, Zhuge, and Liu Ji. *Mastering the Art of War*. Trans. Thomas Cleary. Boston: Shambhala, 1989.

Musashi, Miyamoto. *A Book of Five Rings*. Trans. Victor Harris. New York: Overlook Press, 1974.

Musashi, Miyamoto. *The Book of Five Rings*. Trans. Nihon Services Corp. New York: Bantam Books, 1982.

Musashi, Miyamoto. *The Book of Five Rings*. Trans. Thomas Cleary. Boston: Shambhala, 1993.

Noguchi, Isamu. *Essays and Conversations*. New York: Harry N. Abrams, 1994.

Oh, Sadaharu, and David Falkner. *A Zen Way of Baseball*. New York: Vintage Books, 1984.

Reps, Paul. *Zen Flesh, Zen Bones*. New York: Anchor Books, 1961.

Sekida, Katsuku. *Two Zen Classics*. New York: Weatherhill, 1977.

Sen, Soshitsu XV. *Tea Life, Tea Mind*. New York: Weatherhill, 1979.

Shimano, Eido Tai, and Kogetsu Tani. *Zen Word, Zen Calligraphy*. Boston: Shambhala, 1990.

Soho, Takuan. *The Unfettered Mind*. Tokyo: Kodansha International, 1986.

Sun Tzu. *The Art of War*. Trans. Samuel B. Griffith. London: Oxford University Press, 1963.

Sun Tzu. Ed. James Clavell. *The Art of War*. New York: Dell Publishing, 1983.

Sun Tzu. *The Art of War*. Trans. Thomas Cleary. Boston: Shambhala, 1988.

Suzuki, Shunryu. *Zen Mind, Beginner's Mind*. New York: Weatherhill, 1970.

Ueshiba, Kisshomaru. *The Spirit of Aikido*. Tokyo: Kodansha International, 1984.

Yamamoto, Tsunetomo. *Hagakure*. Trans. William Scott Wilson. Tokyo: Kodansha International, 1979.

Yasuda, Kenneth. *The Japanese Haiku*. Tokyo: Charles E. Tuttle, 1957.

Yoshikawa, Eiji. *Musashi: The Art of War*. New York: Pocket Books, 1971.

Yoshikawa, Eiji. *Musashi: The Bushido Code*. New York: Pocket Books, 1971.

Yoshikawa, Eiji. *Musashi: The Way of Life and Death*. New York: Pocket Books, 1971.

Yoshikawa, Eiji. *Musashi: The Way of the Samurai*. New York: Pocket Books, 1971.

Yoshikawa, Eiji. *Musashi: The Way of the Sword*. New York: Pocket Books, 1971.

Yoshioka, Toichi. *Zen*. Osaka: Hoikusha Publishing, 1978.

THE QUOTATIONS in this book came from the following sources:

Beginner's Mind

Jimi Hendrix: Scott Isler, "Jimi Hendrix in His Own Words," *Musician* (November 1991): 32–46.

The Edge: Tom Nolan and Jas Obrecht, "The Edge of U2," *Guitar Player* (June 1985): 54–68, 89.

Frank Zappa: *The Guitar Player Book, Revised and Updated*, 3rd ed. (New York: Grove Press, Inc., 1983), 302–310.

Joni Mitchell: Chip Stern, "Joni Mitchell Pulls Your Ear," *Musician* (January–February 1995): 22–31.

Brian Eno: Kevin Kelly, "Gossip Is Philosophy," *Wired* (May 1995): 146–151, 204–209.

Practice

Chet Atkins: *The Guitar Player Book,* 1–10.

Dizzy Gillespie: Chip Stern, "Diggin' Diz," *Musician* (March 1992): 46–53.

Stone Gossard: Vic Garbarini, "Mother of Pearl," *Musician* (May 1995): 52–60.

Pat Martino: *The Guitar Player Book,* 168–170.

Manu Katché: Tony Scherman, "Manu Katché's French Cooking," *Musician* (March 1993): 73–74.

Townes Van Zandt: Bill Flanagan, "Ragged Company," *Musician* (August 1995): 30–43, 68.

Joe Pass: *The Guitar Player Book*, 211–13.

Paul McCartney: "Beatles," *Musician* (July 1995): 26–27, 32–33.

Steve Vai: James Rotondi, "Star Man," *Guitar Player* (May 1995): 84–102.

Chet Atkins: *The Guitar Player Book,* 1–10.

Joan Baez: Mike Sager, "Joan Baez," *Rolling Stone* (November 5–December 10, 1987): 162–164.

Joshua Redman: Karen Bennett, "Frontman: Joshua Redman," *Musician* (April 1995): 7.

Jimmy Page: "Turning Over a New Leaf," *Guitar for the Practicing Musician* (March 1985): 48–51, 60, 68.

Neil Young: Mark Rowland, "Young Buck!" *Musician* (April 1993): 42–53.

Johnny Winter: *The Guitar Player Book*, 295–299.

John McLaughlin: Chris Gill, James Rotondi, and Jas Obrecht, "Within You Without You: The Guitarist's Search for Spiritual Meaning," *Guitar Player* (May 1995): 48–58.

Carlos Santana: Richard Johnston, "Demons, Angels, and the Holy Boogie," *Best of Guitar Player: Santana/Beck* (October 1995): 8–16.

Woody Guthrie: Woody Guthrie, *Bound for Glory* (New York: E. P. Dutton & Co., 1943), 222.

Les Paul: *The Guitar Player Book,* 214–220.

Edward Van Halen: Mark Rowland, "Twilight of the Guitar Gods," *Musician* (March 1995): 40–48.

Jerry Garcia: *The Guitar Player Book,* 95–100.

Tom Petty: Mark Rowland, "Heartbreaker Straight Ahead," *Musician* (September 1987): 78–86.

Jeff Beck: *The Guitar Player Book*, 14–21.

Gary Bartz: Mark Rowland, et. al. "Sketches of Miles," *Musician* (December 1991): 37–50.

Paul Westerberg: David Wild, "Paul Westerberg," *Rolling Stone* (November 17, 1994), 106–107.

Responsibility

Eric Clapton: "Eric Clapton," *Musician* (July 1995): 38–39, 43.

Frank Zappa: "Frank Zappa," *Musician* (July 1995): 34, 42.

The Edge: Bill Flanagan, "The View From the Edge," *Musician* (March 1992): 56–64.

Robbie Robertson: Bill Flanagan, "The Return of Robbie Robertson," *Musician* (September 1987): 88–98, 113.

Pat Metheny: Josef Woodard, "Breaking Through to Pat Metheny," *Musician* (September 1995): 30–40.

George Benson: *The Guitar Player Book,* 22–23.

Joe Pass: *The Guitar Player Book,* 211–213.

Brian Eno: Kevin Kelly, "Gossip Is Philosophy," *Wired* (May 1995): 146–151, 204–209.

Tom Hamilton: John Stix, "Aerosmith Feel the Burn," *Guitar For the Practicing Musician* (May 1993): 83–96, 129, 145.

Joe Strummer: Dev Sherlock, "Frontman: Joe Strummer," *Musician* (June 1995): 7.

Keith Richards: "Rolling Stones," *Musician* (July 1995): 66–67, 83–85.

Henry Kaiser: Ted Drozdowski, "Gonzo Guitarists & the Big Whack(o) Attack," *Musician* (September 1987): 46–50.

Miles Davis: "Miles Davis," *Musician* (July 1995): 48–49.

Andrés Segovia: *The Guitar Player Book,* 241–248.

Miles Davis: "Miles Davis," *Musician* (July 1995): 48–49.

Stevie Ray Vaughn: "Stevie Ray Vaughn," *Musician* (July 1995): 88, 94.

Keith Richards: Kurt Loder, "Keith Richards," *Rolling Stone* (November 5–December 10, 1987): 64–67.

Buster Williams: Mark Rowland, et. al. "Sketches of Miles," *Musician* (December 1991): 37–50.

Bill Kirchen: Chris Gill, "Profile: Bill Kirchen," *Guitar Player* (May 1995): 41–42.

Rick Danko: Kevin Ransom, "The Band's Shout Across the Great Divide," *Guitar Player* (May 1995): 75–81.

B. B. King: *The Guitar Player Book,* 147–150.

Branford Marsalis: "Wynton & Branford Marsalis," *Musician* (July 1995): 70–71, 94.

Duke Ellington: Nat Hentoff, *Miles Davis: The Columbia Years 1955–85* (CBS Records Inc., 1988): liner notes.

Eric Clapton: *The Guitar Player Book,* 64–67.

Buddy Guy: Jas Obrecht, "Buddy Guy: The Happiest Man Alive," *Guitar Player* (June 1993): 86–96.

Carlos Santana: Jas Obrecht, "Carlos Santana," *Guitar Player* (January 1988): 46–54.

Allan Holdsworth: *The Guitar Player Book,* 109–115.

Barrier

Bruce Springsteen: Mikal Gilmore, "Bruce Springsteen," *Rolling Stone* (November 5–December 10, 1987): 22–26.

Henry Threadgill: Jim Macine, "Global Jelly Roll with the Bismarck of Jazz," *Musician* (April 1995): 40–49.

Neil Young: Tony Scherman, "Frontman: Neil Young," *Musician* (December 1991): 7.

Ringo Starr: "Beatles," *Musician* (July 1995): 26–27, 32–33.

David Torn: Chris Gill, James Rotondi, and Jas Obrecht, "Within You Without You: The Guitarist's Search for Spiritual Meaning," *Guitar Player* (May 1995): 48–58.

George Harrison: Bill Flanagan, "The Dark Horse Candidate," *Musician* (September 1992): 40–48.

Bob Dylan: Kurt Loder, "Bob Dylan," *Rolling Stone* (November 5–December 10, 1987): 301–303.

Acknowledgments

Heartfelt thanks go to:

My mother and father, for starting me off on the path;

Rich and Paul, for walking with me;

Salvatore Principato, for sharing his huge spirit and all that Avant Garbage;

John Berenzy, for his noble heart;

Steve Scavuzzo, for changing the course of my life;

Chas Schreier, for jammin' and truckin';

Kim Milai, for the beat, and Patrick Derivaz, for never wasting time;

Bryan Brown, for making me think;

Ken Hiratsuka, for drawing that one line;

Lee Kravitz, for his commitment to excellence;

Steven Manning, for sharing the love of music;

Bob Mould, for the spark;

Ronald Ross, for caring about every word;

Renee Glaser, for catching everything;

Master Dong Jin Kim, for steeling me on the true path;

Carol Reitz, for her vital early critique;

Marc Stern, for the third chord;

HAC, Mold, and Jay Wasco, for the fun and the noise;

David Oliver Relin, for the sage advice;

Gini Sikes, for the crucial help;

My agents, Laurie Fox and Linda Chester, for believing I had something to say;

My editor, Mary Ann Naples, for her enthusiasm
and mindfulness;
All my teachers, for all the lessons.

Most of all, thanks to Tracy, for the love, support, and wealth of
insights that made this book so much better;
and Naomi, for the constant inspiration.
You light my life every minute of every day.
How did I ever get so lucky?

Author Contact

Recordings of the author's music and other Zen Guitar stuff are available by writing:

The Zen Guitar Dojo
P.O. Box 385278
Minneapolis, MN 55438
USA

Comments and inquiries are also welcome via electronic mail: zen_gtr@maui.net

Visit the Zen Guitar home page on the World Wide Web at: http://www.maui.net/~zen_gtr

About the Author

Philip Toshio Sudo began playing the guitar as a child in Japan. He developed the Zen Guitar philosophy performing in the streets, parks, and subways of New York City, and in 1993 became an official musician of the New York City Marathon. He lives with his wife and children in Maui, Hawaii, where he writes and records his music.